Parents, Their Children, and Schools

Parents, Their Children, and Schools

EDITED BY

Barbara Schneider
and James S. Coleman

Westview Press

BOULDER • SAN FRANCISCO • OXFORD

This book was supported by a grant from the National Science Foundation and The National Center for Education Statistics (SES-8803225), principal investigator James S. Coleman. The opinions expressed herein are those of the authors and not the sponsoring agencies.

Published in 1993 in the United States of America by Westview Press, Inc., 5500 Central Avenue, Boulder, Colorado 80301-2877, and in the United Kingdom by Westview Press, 36 Lonsdale Road, Summertown, Oxford OX2 7EW

Library of Congress Cataloging-in-Publication Data
Parents, their children, and schools / edited by Barbara Schneider and
    James S. Coleman
        p.   cm.
    Includes bibliographical references and index.
    ISBN 0-8133-1639-1
    1. Home and school—United States—Longitudinal studies.
2. Education—United States—Parent participation—Longitudinal
studies.   I. Schneider, Barbara, 1946–   . II. Coleman, James
Samuel, 1926–   .
LC225.3.P38   1993
649'.68—dc20   93-3720
                                                                      CIP

Printed and bound in the United States of America

The paper used in this publication meets the requirements
of the American National Standard for Permanence of Paper
for Printed Library Materials Z39.48-1984.

10   9   8   7   6   5   4   3   2

Contents

6 Parent Choice and Inequality 147
James S. Coleman, Kathryn S. Schiller, and Barbara Schneider

Tables and Figures

Tables

Figures

Acknowledgments

During the course of this work, several individuals made important contributions. We gratefully acknowledge the helpful contributions of the following people: Charles Bidwell, Anthony Bryk, Joyce Epstein, Adam Gamoran, Maureen Hallinan, James MacPartland, Milbrey McLaughlin, Stephen Plank, MariLi Pooler, Jennifer Schmidt, Bruce Spencer, David Stevenson, Joan Talbert, Ogburn Stouffer Education Studies Group, and Hendrickson Creative Communications.

Barbara Schneider
James S. Coleman

1

Parents, Their Children, and Schools: An Introduction

Barbara Schneider

One of the most important factors in a child's success in school is the degree to which his or her parents are actively involved in the child's education. Yet, we really know very little about those actions parents take with their children at home, in school, and in the community that actually improve school performance. For example, will a mother help her child more by working full-time for extra income or by staying home and supervising the child after school? What are some parents depriving their children of by not contacting the school regularly? If parents know the parents of their child's friends, can this compensate for a lack of time and money spent on the child?

Not all parents have the same resources or opportunities to act on the educational expectations they have for their children. Variations in financial and social resources, such as money to purchase a home computer or adequate child care, factor into parents' decisions about the actions they take regarding their children's education. Family composition, that is, the number of adults in the household and their relationships to the children, constitutes another social resource, the nature of which can affect educational opportunities in the home. Similarly, the absence of a parent may negatively impact a child's learning environment. For example, in families where there is only one parent, household duties like cooking, cleaning, and attending to child care may limit the amount of time that can be devoted to helping a child with homework. Furthermore, if the single parent has a full-time job, this may further reduce the amount of unrestricted time the adult has to spend with the child.

Parent involvement in a child's education is also affected by the opportunities made available by the school. Some schools may encourage parents to contact teachers about their children's academic performance, social development, or future plans such as selecting a high school program and courses. Other schools may have certain policies or characteristics that discourage parents from contacting the school regarding their children's academic achievement or high school plans. Schools with these policies may offer few activities, such as parent-teacher conferences, go-to-school nights, or fund-raising events, that foster communication and social ties between families and school personnel.

Community characteristics, such as informal networks among parents, are another resource for increasing parent involvement. For example, if parents frequently interact, they can share information about their children, their children's teachers, new school policies, and they can express their complaints about the school. These networks can generate either positive or negative opinions about various aspects of school life and serve as a vehicle for bringing issues to school boards and school administrators.

Parent involvement, then, is shaped by parents' orientation toward education, their financial and social resources, and the opportunities that are available in the schools and communities in which they live. This book is designed to look at the resources that parents have and the actions that they take in their children's education. It is a story of different types of families—two-parent families, single parents, working mothers, some with high incomes and high levels of education, some that are very poor economically, some that have high educational expectations for their children, others who do not, families of different racial and ethnic groups—and how they are involved in their children's education and what effect it has on student performance. It is a story of what these families do at home, at school, and in the community to facilitate their children's achievement.

Interest in Families

The roles the American family and school can have in the education of our children demand systematic inquiry, especially given the dramatic changes occurring in these social institutions. Traditional families, or those composed of mother, father, and child, represent a much smaller proportion of American households today than in the past. Nearly half of all American children under the age of 18 will be raised in single parent homes, arising from a divorce or separation at one time in their lives (Statistical Abstract of the United States 1991). These rates are even higher for African American children, the majority of whom will be raised in single parent homes.

Today, mothers are entering the labor force in increasing numbers. From 1970 to 1989 the number of mothers working outside the home increased by more than 20% (Statistical Abstract of the United States 1991). The rise in labor force participation has been greater for those women with children than for those with no children. Today, most mothers will work outside the home for a significant part of their children's school years.

Arguably, the rise in the number of working mothers has also decreased the amount of time mothers can spend with their children, thus leaving supervision to other child care institutions. Oftentimes the values adopted in these child care facilities and the children who attend them may be in direct conflict with those reinforced in the home. Receiving different messages about what constitutes good behavior at school, how to treat teachers and peers, and why schooling is important, many children find they have to cope with these contradictions in values by themselves.

The growth in the number of two-income families has increased the amount of discretionary income in many households. Some modern families seem to invest more in their children than was once the case, not merely in terms of money, but also in time and attention. Of course, this is not the case in all situations, as there are other parents who, regardless of their income, are narcissistic and neglectful toward their children. Many schools have to contend with a mass of families who are willing and able to expend considerable resources on their children while dealing with families who are unable or unwilling to do so.

Like families, schools have also undergone major structural changes. The growth of school districts and the professionalization of the teachers have in many instances distanced schools from the families and communities they once served. The distance between families and schools is further exacerbated by television, another potent force that has become a significant actor in the life of children. The commercial world has aggressively sought to compete with families and schools for children's time and monetary resources.

Families have few mechanisms to insulate their children from the messages communicated through the media. Schools also lack such mechanisms. The school, not unlike the family, is not currently organized to compete successfully against the external conditions of this commercial world. This world offers children yet another set of values which are often contradictory to those of the school and the family.

Perhaps now more than ever, families find themselves needing support and sustenance from schools to help them in the education of their children. Schools also need the support and sustenance provided by the family to make this possible. The question then becomes, how can families and schools work together for the benefit of children in our modern society?

The study of family-school relations has been dominated by educators and sociologists, both bring their own perspectives to bear on the problem. Educational researchers have been primarily concerned with identifying parent activities at home and in school that help preschoolers and elementary students improve their cognitive and social development skills (Leichter 1978). Focusing on "readiness," many of these studies explore how parents can prepare their young children for school. Studies with older students have tended to concentrate on assisting parents in improving the academic performance of their children through such activities as engaging in ongoing communication with school professionals and monitoring homework and other out-of-school assignments (Epstein 1987; Baker and Stevenson 1986).

Social scientists concerned with family-school relations have tended to view the contribution of the family to the child's academic performance through socio-demographic factors, such as who is in the home, what type of jobs household members have, and the quality of the child care provided to younger children. They focus on these factors as well as family occupational status, income, and educational attainment, but typically do not focus on the processes by which some families support and create opportunities for learning (Coleman 1988).

More recently, educators and sociologists have turned their attention to family beliefs, activities, and cultural values to gain an understanding of how some families become involved with their child's school (Clark 1983; Lareau 1989). Recognizing that families vary in their economic resources and attitudes toward education, these researchers have concentrated on describing variations in family values and the types of activities families feel comfortable pursuing in schools. Primarily qualitative in their methodological approach, these studies are somewhat constrained in their ability to make systematic connections between parent actions and student academic outcomes.

From a policy perspective, research on parent involvement in schools has tended to focus on relating family background characteristics to school involvement activities and then tracing that involvement to achievement. The underlying assumption is that parent involvement, especially for minorities, can counteract the negative effects of low socioeconomic background and significantly improve student performance. But the drawback of this approach is that it tends to define parent involvement through school-based activities, such as joining parent-teacher organizations, serving on advisory boards, or helping with homework, rather than using a more holistic definition, looking at parent involvement in the home and community and relating that to specific school characteristics.

In contrast to these views, we are interested in isolating both the values parents have and the actions they take in the home toward the education of their children that may increase academic performance and social development. We are interested in determining what norms and sanctions families impose that encourage or discourage learning in school and what other social institutions families use besides formal schools to socialize and reinforce children's learning. If we are to better understand variation in how families educate their children, we need to look more closely at the values and activities undertaken by families.

We approach this problem by focusing on the social and economic resources of the family and then by looking specifically within the home, community and school to learn how families are involved in educational activities. Our analyses begin by isolating family social and economic resources that are likely to encourage or prevent families from supporting their child's education. However, our analyses do not end with first order explanations but move to examine those intervening activities that parents can pursue to compensate for the lack of certain resources, like time. Networking with other parents can be especially beneficial for single mothers as they can learn more about the school, such as which teachers are especially problematic for boys or girls, which ones assign and grade homework, and who are the best mathematics or English teachers.

We maintain that there are a variety of activities that parents undertake to help their children learn, not all of which are formally tied to the school. For example, some parents may enroll their child in music classes outside of the school. The discipline and time involved in learning an instrument can have positive spillover effects on other academic work. The actions parents take at home with their children can be seen as a measure of their responsiveness to the availability of certain resources. From our perspective, parents' decisions to spend time talking to their children about school or implement rules about television viewing and homework constitute means through which parents conceivably can positively influence children's learning. Both time and communication help to strengthen social relations between parents and their children.

There may in addition be orientations and actions of parents that are important for a child's education quite apart from the time spent with the child, or relations with the school or with other parents. Some parents, for example, hold strong expectations and make strong demands concerning their child's school performance, while others do not. Children know what is expected in terms of effort and performance, with or without extensive communication with their parents about school matters.

Social Resources in the Family

The changes in the structure of the American family will undoubtedly influence how educational values are communicated and supported among family members. We assume that social control in families is typically maintained through authority and norms, provided that conditions necessary to uphold the source of that authority and the norms are present. Norms and authority in families, as well as communities, are developed and sustained through relationships. These relationships can form a source of social capital, that is, those social resources in the family and in the community which serve as capital assets available to members of the family. These resources are particularly valuable as they can serve as a conduit through which norms, standards and expectations are conveyed (for further discussion of social capital see Coleman (1990)).

The closer and denser the relationships, the more likely they are to act as constraints upon behavior. A family that is very close or a community that is characterized by many relations of interdependence will have extensive norms and clearly delineated sanctions which serve to control deviant actions by its members. A more loosely constructed family or a community whose interactions are casual and incidental will have fewer and more ambiguous norms and sanctions.

Recognizing that families have these potential assets, we are interested in learning what actions help to accumulate additional capital within the home. Thus, our first priority is to investigate how social capital forms in the home and the community and its relationship to strengthening student academic performance. From the family and community we move to the school, recognizing that most policies directed at encouraging greater involvement on the part of parents in their children's education will be constructed around schools. However, we have relatively limited information concerning what types of schools encourage parent involvement or, for that matter, what types of activities schools use to involve parents and what effect they have on performance.

Parents make choices about the type of actions they are willing to engage in at home, in the community, and in the school that relate both directly and indirectly to their children's education. These choices are influenced by family economic and social constraints as well as by the policies and practices in the schools their children attend. For example, a family decision to contact the school regarding their child's academic performance will be influenced by the parents' assessment of the child's performance, their knowledge of school policies regarding making such contacts, and the resources needed to make the contact, such as getting time off from work or hiring a baby-sitter. Immigrant families may be less willing to contact the school because they may not know the procedures for doing so or how such actions are viewed by the school and teachers. On the other hand, in close communities where such activities are fairly commonplace, families who do not contact the school may be perceived by the school as being uninterested in their child's education.

School choice represents another form of parent involvement that has received considerable attention from scholars and policy makers. During the last decade we have learned a great deal about the families who exercise school choice in the private sector and the educational experiences their children receive in different types of schools (Coleman and Hoffer 1987; Coleman, Hoffer, and Kilgore 1982). Two questions remain however. First, exercising choice represents an effective social resource for improving student performance, taking into account other resources such as parents' education. Second, it is unclear who would take advantage of school choice if choice were expanded in both the private and public sectors. Thus, it is important to learn the impact of school choice opportunities on student outcomes and on equality of educational opportunities.

Furthermore, the effort to understand the actions that parents take with their children has yet to have the benefit of large-scale survey data. For example, studies at the elementary school level which look at family resources and parent involvement have primarily been conducted on small samples and have been of a qualitative nature. From these efforts, we have learned about the significance of helping with homework, the importance of a place to study, and the effect of parent participation in school activities on student performance. The difficulty with these types of studies, however, is that it is nearly impossible to control for variations in family resources such as income, parent education, family composition, or the effects of racial and ethnic discrimination.

Data Base and Sample Selection

The National Education Longitudinal Study of 1988 (NELS:88), a national random sample of 26,000 eighth graders and their parents, teachers, and school administrators, provides us with a data base of information on parent involvement. Conducted by the National Center for Education Statistics (NCES), NELS:88 is the third in a series of national longitudinal studies of American students that began in 1972. NELS:88 differs from other longitudinal studies in that the first data collection phase occurred when the students were in eighth grade. A substantial subsample of the NELS:88

students were resurveyed in 1990 as sophomores, and in 1992 when they were high school seniors. The two previous NCES studies, in 1972 and 1980, began when the students were in secondary school and followed them through post secondary school into adulthood.

Substantively, NELS:88 was designed to examine student achievement over time and to focus on family, community, school, and classroom factors that may promote or inhibit educational success. Specific issues addressed by NELS:88 which were consistent with our interests include: the number of adults in the home, the relationship between these adults, parents' employment status, parents' investments in out-of-school educational activities such as computer and music classes, parents' knowledge of the parents of their child's friends, incidence of contact between parents and schools, and parents' participation in parent-teacher organizations (PTO). Further, NELS:88 includes data on what high school a student was likely to attend and what other schools, if any, the student was considering.

The NELS:88 base year study collected data from students, parents, teachers, and school administrators. Self-administered questionnaires and tests represented the principal modes of data collection. The student questionnaire solicited information on basic demographic variables and on a range of other topics including schoolwork, aspirations, and social relationships. Students also completed a series of curriculum-based cognitive tests. One parent of each student was asked to respond to a parent survey which gauged parent aspirations for their children, family willingness to commit resources to their children's education, home educational rules and supports, and other family characteristics related to achievement. Two teachers of each sampled student also completed a teacher questionnaire designed to collect data about teacher evaluations of selected students, course content and classroom teaching practices, and school and teacher characteristics. A school administrator questionnaire completed by the school principal requested information about the school's teaching staff, the school's climate, characteristics of the student body, and school policies and offerings.

The base year survey employed a two-stage, stratified sample design. The first stage of sample selection involved the schools, and the second stage focused on the students within the selected schools. To ensure a balanced sample, schools were first stratified by region, urbanicity, and percentage of minorities prior to sampling. The school sample consisted of public and private schools (including independent, Catholic, and other types of religious schools) with eighth graders. Schools considered ineligible were those that served special student populations, such as the Bureau of Indian Affairs schools, special education schools for the handicapped, and schools for dependents of U.S. personnel overseas. From a national frame encompassing 39,000 schools with eighth graders, a total of 1,057 schools participated in the study.

Within each school approximately 26 students were randomly selected. In sampled schools with fewer than 24 eighth graders, all eligible students were selected. In schools where 26 students were surveyed, there were 24 regularly sampled students. Two additional Hispanic and Asian/Pacific Islander students were also included. (For a complete description of the base year sample design, see Spencer, Frankel, Ingels, Rasinski, and Tourangeau, NELS:88 Base Year Sample Design Report 1990.)

Profile of the Sample

The oversample of Hispanics and Asian Americans makes the NELS:88 study particularly valuable for examining racial and ethnic differences in parental resources and involvement, and student achievement among various racial and ethnic groups. To gain an initial picture of the NELS:88 student sample, Table 1.1 presents several key family characteristics and student outcome measures disaggregated by race and ethnicity. Percentages displayed in Table 1.1 are calculated based on a weighted sample scaled to match the size of the unweighted sample (see the NELS:88 Base Year Sample Design Report 1990 for further discussion of the weighting formulae).[1]

Looking at family composition, we see that 78% of Asian American students are living with both natural parents. African American students represent the other extreme, with only 38% living with both natural parents. African American students are more than twice as likely as the sample as a whole to be living with a single mother. About two thirds of Hispanic (63%) and white (68%) students live with both natural parents. Whereas single parent homes appear to be the most common alternative family type for African Americans, stepfamilies appear to be as common as single parent homes for Asian American, Hispanic and white students.

Size of family also varies by race and ethnicity. The largest number of siblings living at home is found among Native American and Hispanic families. Native Americans and Hispanics are likely to be living in homes with three or more siblings. White students, on average, live in homes with the fewest siblings (averaging 2.46 per family).

Variations by race and ethnicity are also apparent with respect to family income and parent education. The median family income for Asian Americans and whites is more than double that of African Americans ($36,035 and $34,264 versus $16,430). The median family income for Hispanic students ($20,305) is 60% of that of whites.

TABLE 1.1 Descriptive statistics for total sample by race/ethnicity

	All	Asian American	Hispanic	African American	White	Native American
Sample n	24,599	1,527	3,171	3,009	16,317	299
Weighted percent of sample	100.00	3.50	10.40	13.20	71.60	1.30
Head of family (%)						
Both natural parents	63.73	78.31	63.49	38.33	67.88	54.86
Natural and stepparent	14.13	7.45	13.13	15.14	14.41	14.06
Single mother	16.39	8.39	17.72	36.08	12.89	21.36
Single father	2.43	2.24	2.12	2.70	2.70	3.33
Other	3.17	3.52	3.42	8.32	2.12	6.39
Number of students in household (mean)	2.6	2.7	3.0	2.7	2.5	3.3
Household income (median)	$30,690	$36,035	$20,305	$16,430	$34,264	$20,726
Education of at least 1 parent (%)						
High school graduate	89.60	91.23	66.65	84.23	93.81	86.61
4-year college graduate	26.64	45.76	12.43	13.62	30.30	16.19
Grades quartiles (%)						
Low	24.81	16.45	30.57	28.80	23.45	36.71
2	22.20	16.16	24.50	28.29	20.95	27.63
3	24.60	21.28	25.25	26.30	24.39	23.07
High	28.39	46.11	19.68	16.60	31.22	12.59
Test score composite quartiles (%)						
Low	24.76	19.39	40.41	49.13	17.96	45.94
2	24.35	21.27	28.80	27.39	23.21	30.52
3	25.91	23.58	20.43	16.57	28.69	15.75
High	24.98	35.76	10.36	6.91	30.14	7.79
Urbanicity of school (%)						
Urban	25.05	34.68	40.53	50.30	17.58	29.67
Suburban	43.79	52.67	39.88	27.94	47.06	32.40
Rural	31.16	12.65	19.60	21.76	35.36	37.93

Parent education follows a somewhat parallel pattern. Forty-six percent of the Asian American students have one parent with a college degree or higher. Thirty percent of white students have one parent with that level of education. In contrast, 12% and 14% of the Hispanic and African American students, respectively, have parents with these educational attainment levels. Hispanics are the most likely to have at least one parent who did not graduate from high school.

The distribution of teacher-awarded grades by student racial and ethnic groups also shows large differences. Forty-six percent of Asian American students and 31% of white students have grades in the highest quartile compared to 19.7% of the Hispanics and 16.6% of the African Americans. These results are reversed when examining the lowest grade quartile. Thirty-one percent of Hispanics followed by 28.8% of African Americans receive grades in the lowest grade categories.

Examining the composite achievement test scores, we find that over a third of the Asians (35.7%) and slightly less than a third the of whites (30.1%) have composite achievement test scores in the highest quartile. In contrast, 7% of African Americans, 8% of Native Americans and 10% of Hispanics have test scores in the highest quartile. Racial and ethnic differences in composite test scores remain even when the educational level of the parents is held constant.[2]

As for school location, African Americans and Hispanics are most likely to attend schools in urban areas, Asian Americans and whites are most likely to attend suburban schools, and Native Americans are most likely to attend rural schools.

Overview of the Findings

The remainder of this volume is organized into five chapters. Chapter 2 provides a general overview of selected forms of parent involvement in the home, school, and community. We find that different racial and ethnic groups vary in the types of involvement they have with their children. For example, Asian Americans tend not to be involved in school related activities such as parent-teacher organizations (PTO). In contrast to other racial and ethnic groups, Asian American parents spend considerably more resources on education-related activities outside of school such as music and computer lessons.

The relationship among family composition, parent involvement, and student outcomes is described in Chapter 3. Families with both natural parents are the most successful in promoting student achievement test scores and grades. These results take into account differing family backgrounds such as parental education, family income, and race and ethnicity.

Chapter 4 looks at the effect of maternal employment on parent involvement and student outcomes. Families in which the mother works part-time tend to be more involved in encouraging their children to be successful in school. Children whose mothers are employed part-time tend to score higher on achievement tests and those whose mothers are either employed part-time or not in the labor force receive higher grades.

How schools facilitate or inhibit parent involvement, especially school-based involvement, is examined in Chapter 5. Parental involvement is most effective by the presence or absence of family resources including mother's employment status, parent education levels, and family composition and income. While most parents demonstrate concern regarding their children's education, the lack of resources can be a major obstacle to being involved in school activities. However, African American and Hispanic parents manage to compensate for limited resources and exhibit higher rates of involvement in the school when compared to white parents of similar background characteristics.

Finally, Chapter 6 examines which parents take advantage of school choice opportunities in either the public or private sectors and what effect expanded choice might have for increasing equality of educational opportunity for disadvantaged students. Our analyses suggest that educational disadvantages due to race and ethnicity are different than those created by low parental education levels. For example, African Americans show a high propensity to respond to expansion of school choice in the public sector. Parents with low education levels demonstrate a deeper form of disadvantage; they show less investment in their childrens' education than those parents with more years of schooling even when controlling for family income.

Notes

1. All of the analyses in this volume are conducted on a weighted sample.

2. The complete analyses regarding grades, race and ethnicity, and parent education can be found in Chapter 4.

2

Parent Involvement in the Home, School, and Community

Chandra Muller and David Kerbow

Children's success in school depends greatly on their family background. Family background is so important it even influences how a student utilizes the resources available from school. Beyond the child's own background, the combined backgrounds of the students in a school affect all the students in that school. In part, family background works the way it does because of the things parents do with and for their child, that is, their involvement with their child and with the process of educating their child.

There are many ways parents might become involved in their children's education. The form parent involvement takes will be shaped by three factors: (1) the resources and opportunities available to the parent (including those provided by the school), (2) the relationship between parent and child, and (3) the interests of parents in the education of the child. The interaction between these components makes the study of how parents are involved in their child's education more complex, because to understand a particular action one must take account of a variety of parameters. To disentangle what parents *do* from what they *have* is essential for understanding the process. This chapter is an initial attempt to describe the various actions parents may take which influence the educational process of their child.

Parent involvement in the child's education may be described in the following way. Families have a defined set of resources. Examples of resources are time, money, the number of parents in the household, and the parents' education. Resources may also be an aspect of the community in which the family lives, such as how well neighbors know each other or what services are available. These resources vary considerably across families, and the manner in which they are made available for the child's education. The interest of the parents in the process of education is likely to shape the ways in which they become involved, that is, how they choose to use their resources and the social relationships they form. The motivation for parents to become involved in their child's education may vary from parent to parent. Some parents may participate in school activities because of a school-associated parent friendship community or as a form of cultural enrichment. Others may view education as the principal means for status attainment. When parents have the view that education will lead to social mobility or status maintenance, the motivation for involvement is readily apparent.

Even an understanding of motivation will not necessarily explain why some parents get involved while others do not. For instance, lack of resources may constrain how parents are able to translate their interests into concrete action. Even if parents expect their child to attend college and have set it as a high priority, financial constraints may prevent them from saving for that future possibility. In addition, the school may play a pivotal role in the connections between parent involvement and the student's educational experience. The school may encourage parent involvement and thus strengthen the positive effects of parent action. By the same token, characteristics of the school, such as school policy or school climate, may make parent involvement more difficult.

The forms parent involvement take, along with the direct influence of family resources and the context of the school, will make a difference in the child's educational experience. That educational experience may be understood by conventional measures of achievement like grades and standardized test scores or other aspects of the process like program enrollment or behavioral problems the student might have. Involvement is likely to be influenced by factors both internal and external to the family. It is within this complex set of influences that we examine the effects of parent involvement on student academic outcomes.

The Context of Parent Involvement

There are different contexts in which parents become involved. They include involvement within the home and family, in the community, and in the school. It is useful to distinguish these contexts for several reasons. The first is that every context, in part, defines the additional actors that may play a role in shaping the action parents take with their child. For example, within the family there is the other parent, other children, and possibly other adults who live in the household. Within the school there are the school personnel, such as the principal and teachers, as well as the school policy or climate, which may encourage or discourage parent participation. Second, findings about parent involvement will have different policy implications depending upon the context. While family resources and the relationship between parent and child will drive or constrain every form of parent involvement, characteristics of the school or the community will constrain or encourage involvement in that particular arena. Thus, policy decisions have to be considered in light of the context of involvement which will be affected.

To conceive of parent involvement as influenced at once by parent resources, parent values, and other relationships between the parent, other parents, and the school is possible only because of the wealth of data in NELS:88. The complexity of the problem and the many interrelationships between the factors we are measuring make a simple description a challenge. Thus, in displaying a basic cross tabulation we must consider many other factors. Our purpose in this chapter is to identify salient questions and to provide a framework for how best to approach these questions concerning parents' involvement in the educational process of their children.

Parents' Expectations for Their Child's Educational Attainment

To understand parent involvement in education it is useful to assess what parents expect their child to take away from the educational process, that is, what their child will accomplish within the system. In large part this is likely to be reflected in the parent's educational expectations for the child. One way to examine this is to analyze parents' expectations for their child relative to the educational attainment of the parents; does the parent anticipate a higher or lower level of attainment for the child? Parents who view education as a means of upward social mobility may have educational expectations for their child that are higher than their own attainment. It may be that parents who think of education as a ticket to upward mobility and aspire to mobility are also more likely to invest in the education of their children. Depending upon the resources available to them, parents might choose different forms of investment, paying for a private school, participating in a parent-teacher organization to improve school conditions, spending time tutoring their child or possibly simply talking about the importance of school with their child.

Figure 2.1 shows the percent of parents with the expectation that their child will go beyond college graduation by the highest level of educational attainment of either parent and by race/ethnicity. Two things are apparent from this figure. First, in general, minority parents with lower levels of education are more likely to expect their child to complete a higher level of

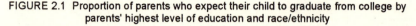

FIGURE 2.1 Proportion of parents who expect their child to graduate from college by
parents' highest level of education and race/ethnicity

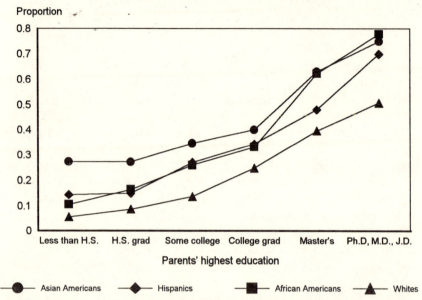

education than their own relative to white parents. This is shown by the gap
between the white curves and the curves for minority groups in areas of the
graph that represent upwardly mobile educational attainment. Second,
highly educated white parents expect their child to attain education levels
lower than their own at a much higher rate than minorities. It seems that
many white parents either expect downward mobility for their children
(which is unlikely) or anticipate the child to maintain their status position
without educational attainment commensurate with the parents. In other
words, many white parents may not feel that earning a higher degree is as
pivotal for enabling their child to either maintain or exceed the social status
of the parents in the same way that minority parents see benefits from
education.

In examining the actions parents take we will consider three contexts of
action. First is the family and home. It is in this context that involvement will
be most influenced by the underlying values and priorities of parents.
Involvement at home is least likely to be constrained by external factors.
Involvement within the home is also most likely to be a reflection of the
fundamental relationship between the parents and child. This includes the
degree to which channels of communication are open and available for
parents to convey their resources, including knowledge, to the child and for
parents to assess the specific needs of the child for those resources.

The second context is the membership of the parent and child in a common community. We do not distinguish the basis of the community; it might be residential, church-based, or school-based. The relevant factor is whether parents know the parents of their children's friends. This form of involvement is constrained not only by the family's resources (e.g., time) but also by the availability of other parents to engage in the activity.

The third and final context is the school. Here parents' actions are constrained or encouraged not only by their personal resources but also by characteristics of the school. School characteristics include the extent to which schools encourage parent participation and the school climate. These may vary with parent participation and characteristics of the student population and school personnel. Each form of parent involvement in a context implies a consideration of the constraints imposed by the other actors in that context.

Home-based Parent Involvement

The structure and character of the child's home environment is in many ways likely to be the most critical area of parent involvement. The parent-child relationship within the home is likely to include a significant historical and cumulative component. Involvement at home is likely to be the least likely to change, since it is the least subject to external constraints. It is also important because it best reflects the nature of the parents' values in education, the ways the educational process is incorporated into the interactions of family members, and how parents structure the child's environment to be conducive to learning. Verbal communication, rules and authority, parent guidance, and parent choice of cultural and educational alternatives will be explored in this section.

Student and Parent Talking. Two kinds of student reported discussion with parents will be examined here: (1) discussion of current school experiences and (2) talking with parents about planning the high school program.[1] Talking about current school experiences has to do with aspects of the current educational process, whereas the second measure (talking about high school program) has to do with future plans and goals. Students report fairly high rates of discussion with parents. Ninety-seven percent of students report talking about school experiences at least once during the past year, and 91% of students report discussing high school program planning with a parent at least once during the past year.

A parent might stress different things in discussions about the educational process depending upon the objectives of the parents for the child's educational experience. Education as cultural enrichment may be reflected more in the discussion of school experiences, whereas discussion of high school program planning may be more occupationally goal directed and motivated by high educational aspirations for the child. These two types of discussion are not mutually exclusive, and the most involved parents are likely to engage heavily in both. Yet they are not necessarily dependent on one another; parents may engage in one and not the other. Also, parents may talk with their child about topics other than those measured here.

On average, whites talk about current experiences at a higher rate than any of the minorities (1.48 for whites compared to 1.38, 1.37, and 1.31 for African Americans, Asian Americans, and Hispanics, respectively).[2] In contrast, African American parents talk about high school program planning at the highest rate (1.35).[3] The remaining subgroups discuss high school program plans at about the same average rate, which is slightly lower than for African Americans, specifically 1.30, 1.29, and 1.27 for whites, Asian Americans, and Hispanics, respectively.

Differences between the subgroups and between the two kinds of talking become more apparent when grades are controlled. Figures 2.2 and 2.3 show the relationship between each of the two kinds of talking, general talk about current school experiences and directed talk with parents about high school program planning, with student grades.[4] The overall trend is one of a strong positive relationship between talking and grades. There is a difference, however, between the racial and ethnic subgroups. At every grade level, whites talk more about current school experiences than any of the racial/ethnic minorities. But, African Americans talk about high school program planning at the highest rates, especially among those who get low grades. When grades are controlled, Asian Americans talk about high school program planning at the lowest rates, with whites and Hispanics in the middle.

These racial and ethnic differences may be due to a number of variations between the groups. Discussion of current aspects of the educational experience may be more likely to come about in families in which parents are able to in some sense "put themselves into the context of the school," figuratively speaking, so that the student and parent have enough commonality of understanding to be able to talk about what happens to the student. When the discussion emphasizes educational planning for the future as opposed to aspects of the current process, the motivation may be instrumental in nature, from a belief on the part of the parents that the educational process is a means of securing a more desirable occupation and life. While there is a clear, positive relationship between grades and communication in all cases, Asian Americans and African Americans show the weakest relationships between grades and the two forms of talking. One might say that high grades are not the motivation for talking among these

FIGURE 2.2 Average level of talking with parents about current school experiences by race/ethnicity and student grades. Data have been smoothed using a moving average.[5]

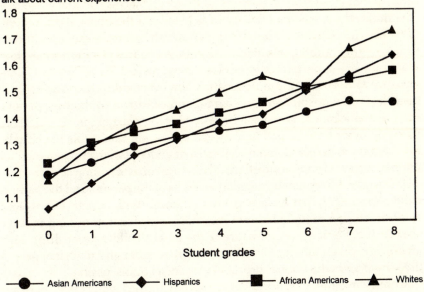

Talk about current experiences

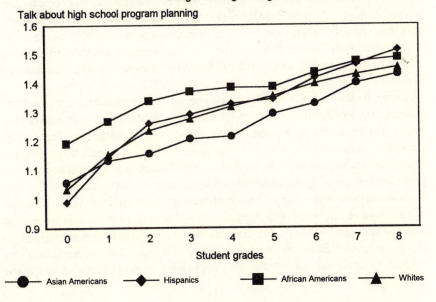

FIGURE 2.3 Average level of talking with parents about high school program planning by race/ethnicity and student grades. Data have been smoothed using a moving average.

Talk about high school program planning

two groups, as they are for whites and Hispanics (although low grades may be a motivation in some cases), or that the effect of talking on the child's performance is greater among whites and Hispanics. The causal direction cannot be determined.

It must be remembered that here, as in most of NELS:88, the measures of parent involvement are of parents' involvement in the educational process. It is entirely possible for parents to be involved with their child while not being particularly involved in the educational process. Each measure of discussion is almost certainly a function of the ongoing (and historical) relationship between parent and child and of the way parents view the educational process. Discussion between parent and child, more than any other form of parent involvement in this data set, is likely to be measuring some basic element of the parent-child relationship represented by an open line of communication.[6] These measures of talking are probably all influenced by some fundamental qualities of the parents and the parent-child relationship that have to do with the ease with which parents and children engage in verbal communication. Each form of talking is topic specific (neither is a pure measure of the parent-child relationship), each include the parent-child relationship, and they differ about what aspect of the school and educational process is the focus of discussion.

Comparing either Figure 2.2 or 2.3 with Figure 2.1 shows that there are clearly different patterns of parental involvement among different ethnic and racial groups. Whites, at every parent education level, are lowest in proportion expecting their child to go beyond a four-year college degree, and Asian American families are highest. Yet this relation is reversed for white parents: At most grade levels, Asian American parents and their children talk least about current school matters or high school programs, while white parents and their children are highest in talking about current school matters, and clearly higher than Asian Americans in talking about high school programs.

Rules. Rules for household behavior represent a form of parent involvement that is wholly distinct from discussion, except that each represents an interest of the parent in the child. It represents a direct effort on the part of parents to impact upon a specific behavior of the child, perhaps with the intention of affecting other behavior as well. For example, a parent may set forth a rule restricting the amount of television the child is allowed to watch on weekdays with the explicit motivation that this restriction will influence the amount of television the child watches. The parent may also think that this will encourage the child to do more homework and thus achieve higher grades in school. Some research has suggested that "family regulation" is related to academic outcomes and especially to deterrence of negative outcomes (c.f. Baumrind 1973; Rumberger et al. 1990). These studies also suggest that the presence of parent-child communication appears to be a factor in the impact of regulation and discipline.[7]

Parent imposed restriction or regulation is an act of intervention, in that it is designed to impact upon a certain behavior. As such it is difficult to make a strong causal argument that the regulatory action causes a behavioral response, such as good grades, from the student. How can we be sure that it is not the behavior of the student that has prompted the parent to intervene? For analysis we have selected two actions parents might take: restricting television watched on weekdays and checking homework. Approximately 45% of the students reported that their parents checked their homework often (compared to 10% who responded never). Only 14% said that their parents often restrict weekday television and 37% reported that they were never restricted.

Figures 2.4 and 2.5 show the relationship of each form of regulation to student reported grades by race and ethnicity. A negative relationship with grades suggests that the action is a form of intervention designed to deter negative outcomes; that is, the parent is responding to a problem of the student.[8] A positive relationship suggests either that the parent responds to positive student behavior with increased involvement or that involvement helps performance. Figure 2.4 indicates a slight positive relationship

FIGURE 2.4 Average level of parent checking homework by student grades and race/ethnicity

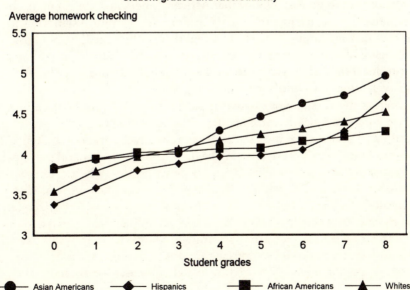

FIGURE 2.5 Average level of parent weekday TV restriction by
student grades and race/ethnicity

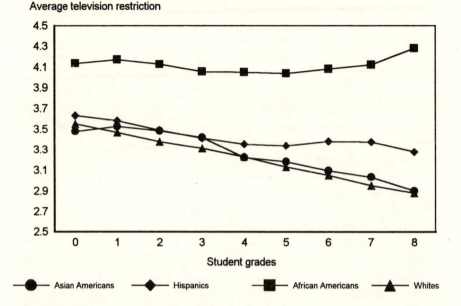

Average television restriction

between student grades and homework checking. It is most pronounced for Asian Americans.

Restricting television, as shown in Figure 2.5, does not have a clear relationship to grades. Notice that African Americans, on average, check homework more frequently, and do so almost uniformly. Asian Americans and whites are similar and show a slightly negative relationship between grades and television restriction. Hispanics restrict television at about the same levels as Asian Americans and whites, but they are more likely to do so even when the child's grades are high.

While the relationship between parent imposed regulation and academic performance is complex, the rules almost certainly influence the child's behavior for which the restriction is directly intended. Figure 2.6 shows that Asian Americans may be the exception. In general they spend much more time on homework than the other groups, whether or not their parents check homework. The time they spend is almost unrelated to the parents' checking of homework. For the other subgroups, as the frequency of parents checking homework increases, so do the hours spent on homework. Similarly, for each group separately, children of parents who restrict television, watch less television (see Figure 2.7). It is the African Americans who spend considerably more time watching television than the others.

FIGURE 2.6 Amount of time student spends on homework per week by
race/ethnicity and frequency parents check homework

Average hours spent on homework per week

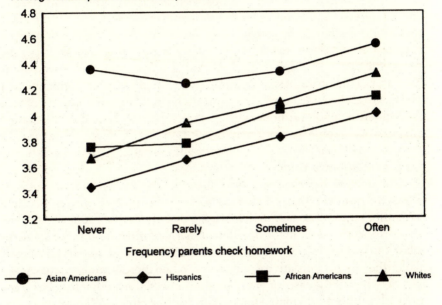

Frequency parents check homework

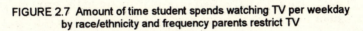

FIGURE 2.7 Amount of time student spends watching TV per weekday
by race/ethnicity and frequency parents restrict TV

Average hours spent watching TV per weekday

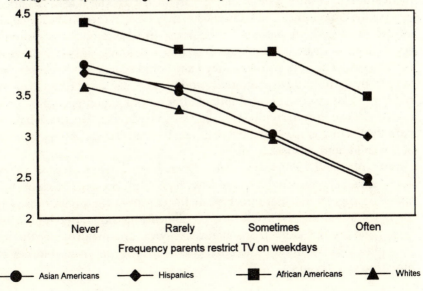

Frequency parents restrict TV on weekdays

With respect to both forms of regulation, the dominant causal relationship is probably that parent action affects student behavior. When parents restrict television, the child watches less television. And when parents check homework, the child spends more time on homework. It is not clear, however, whether these restrictions affect grades or if the relationship is spurious. For example, more involved parents are both more restrictive and have children with higher grades.[9] Perhaps restricting television is an indicator of how conducive the home environment is for academic success. The fact that checking homework is positively related to the amount of time the student spends on homework, but not positively related to grades, suggests that some parents may check homework in response to poor performance (as a form of crisis intervention), while others check homework to maintain a student's good grades.

After School Supervision. One of the most central issues for families in which the mother works outside the home is the question of what the child does after school. The availability of adequate after school supervision may be the deciding factor in the decision of many mothers to enter or leave the labor force. This is likely to be especially true for two-parent families in which there is an alternative wage earner. When there is no alternative wage earner, which is the case for many single mothers, the mother may be forced to work without adequate supervision for her child. Policy makers and school administrators have been slow to respond to the growing need for after school supervision.

After school supervision is different from most other forms of involvement studied, because rather than specifying a provider it asks whether a need of the child is met. This supervision may be provided in the home, the school, or elsewhere, perhaps at the house of a neighbor or community center. In most cases, however, it is the parents' responsibility to arrange for supervision. The opportunities may vary both because available services vary from community to community and the services may be tied to parent resources like income. Availability of after school supervision may influence the decision of the mother to take a job. It embodies the critical balance parents who are employed must maintain between needs of the job, needs of the child, and services available.

Students in NELS:88 were asked, "On average, how much time do you spend after school each day at home with no adult present?" Exploratory analysis suggests that there are three distinct groups of students: those who are never left alone, those who are left alone for less than two hours, and those who are left alone more than two hours. The majority of students (60%) fall into the middle category, those left unsupervised, but not for more than two hours.

Figure 2.8 shows the average grades for students by the amount of time they are left unsupervised. There is a weak relationship between grades and after school supervision. Students who spend more time alone after school have slightly lower grades. Families in which the mother is employed outside the home are the most likely to leave their child unsupervised for long periods of time. Figure 2.9 shows the proportion of parents who leave their children for more than two hours per day by mother's employment status and family composition.[10] It shows that families in which the mother works full-time are most likely to leave their child for long periods, and that among intact families and single mother families the amount of unsupervised time decreases with the time the mother spends employed outside the home.[11] Single mothers are most likely to leave their child unsupervised. In fact, single mothers who are not in the labor force are even more likely to leave their child for long periods than two-parent families in which the mother works full-time.[12]

Single mothers who are employed probably enter the labor force from necessity despite the lack of availability of alternative supervision, thus in part possibly accounting for the higher rates. We see also that stepfather families in which the mother works full-time leave their children at rates closer to those of single mothers than to those of intact families. It is only among stepfamilies in which the mother is employed part-time that the rates of supervision come close to those of intact families.

FIGURE 2.8. Average grades by time spent unsupervised after school

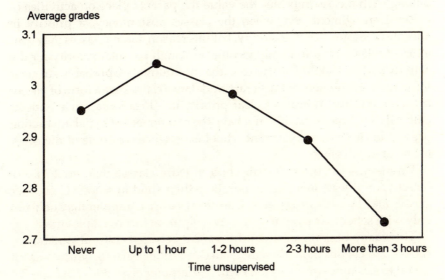

FIGURE 2.9 Proportion of children unsupervised for long periods after school by mother's employment status and family composition

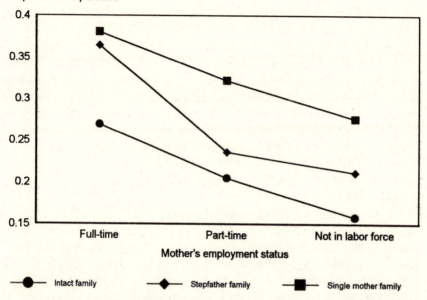

Extra Classes After School. Parents may also choose to send their child to extra classes outside school. Some classes like music, art, and dance may be chosen by parents to provide the child with extra cultural enrichment. Taking such a class indicates the value the parents place on activities of cultural enrichment and, when the classes cost money, a priority in allocating resources to the activity. For this reason, taking classes may bear a direct relationship to family income, although parental priority for the activity and availability of classes in the community are probably stronger influences. Enrollment in music, art, and dance classes are a form of parent involvement that indicates a clear priority in education as an avenue of cultural enrichment but does not have the component of social interaction present in discussion of current school experiences or some of the other forms of involvement.

Parents may also enroll their child in extra classes that would more directly, or at least more obviously, help their child in school. Computer classes may be such an example. Learning to use a computer may help not only with schoolwork but may also be helpful in future employment.

There may be some inherent differences between cultural enrichment classes and classes more directly related to school learning which make it useful to examine enrollment in each. A computer class does not have the cultural appreciation component of a music class; however, the applicability to the improvement of the child's schoolwork is clearer. Also, a major component of music classes is practicing at home; thus, parents must supervise their child's practice. Computer classes (and dance and art classes) do not tend to make as stringent demands on the student's out-of-school time as music classes. It is conceivable that the implied involvement of parents, caused by the practicing demands, is an important component in any effect of music classes.

Figure 2.10 shows the proportion of students enrolled in music class by parents' education and race/ethnicity. Figure 2.11 shows the proportion of students enrolled in computer class by parents' education and race/ethnicity. Very clearly there is a relationship between parents' education and whether the child takes classes outside of school. Asian Americans tend to enroll in both classes at high rates, and whites tend to enroll in music classes, whereas African Americans are more likely to enroll in computer classes. Of course, different availability by community influences the use of these classes. It also, no doubt, indicates how parents of higher educational levels value such activities. Enrollment in extra classes is not only a commitment of money, but also an indication that the child spends time not allocated for schoolwork on other educational activities and, in the case of music classes, practicing. Heyns (1978) suggests that this kind of activity, along with other forms of supplementary education and cultural enrichment, like going to museums, are the kinds of things more highly educated parents do with their children to enhance learning. She also finds that the strategy was a successful one in maintaining and advancing educational gains made in school.

Money Allocated for Education. The money a parent saves for a child's post-secondary education is likely to have a delayed effect on the child, because it will be most useful when the child is faced with post-secondary educational choices. Yet it may be symbolic of parental attitudes, which have an immediate effect on the child. Saving money for education represents a decision on the part of the parent to invest in a future activity rather than to engage in current consumer spending. Furthermore, it implies the placement of a higher value on education by the parents than on other areas in which the money might be spent. Current spending on education represents a predilection of the parents to allocate money toward their child's education. Each type of expenditure indicates an action symbolizing a priority in education.

Figure 2.12 shows the proportion of parents with post-secondary expectations for their child who have started to save money for that child's post-secondary education, by family income and race/ethnicity. Figure 2.13

FIGURE 2.10 Proportion of students enrolled in music outside of school by parents'
highest education and race/ethnicity. Data have been smoothed
using a moving average.

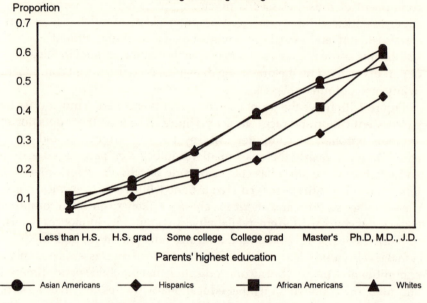

FIGURE 2.11 Proportion of students enrolled in computer outside of school by parents'
highest education and race/ethnicity. Data have been smoothed
using a moving average.

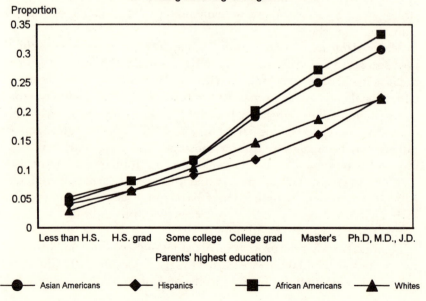

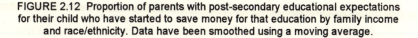

FIGURE 2.12 Proportion of parents with post-secondary educational expectations for their child who have started to save money for that education by family income and race/ethnicity. Data have been smoothed using a moving average.

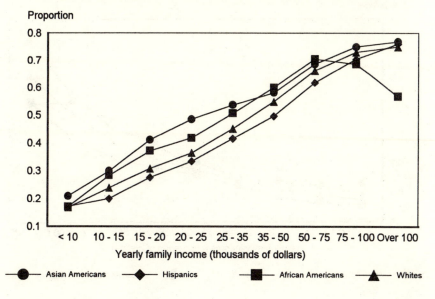

shows the proportion of parents with post-secondary expectations for their child who currently spend money on school tuition and associated expenses, also by family income and race. The measure of saving for post-secondary education is child specific, whereas the measure of current spending is for the family as a unit. In the graphs for Figures 2.12 and 2.13, we see, as one would expect, a strong relationship between income and both savings and spending for education. The relationship with savings is slightly more linear (and the slope is steeper). Notice also that more families save for future education than spend currently.

Although the relative differences among racial/ethnic groups are small, we see that Asian American and African American parents are slightly more likely to have started to save; Asian Americans and Hispanics parents are slightly more likely to spend currently on education. While both measures represent a relatively high value in education held by the parents, the measure of savings is more clearly an action of goal directed involvement. It is more difficult to gauge whether current educational expenditures are motivated by future aspirations or are a response to the immediate educational needs of the child. In both cases, however, we see that minorities are more likely than whites to invest their resources in education. Asian Americans are the most likely to do so.

FIGURE 2.13 Proportion of parents who have post-secondary expectations for their child and currently spend money on tuition and associated expenses by family income and race/ethnicity. Data have been smoothed using a moving average.

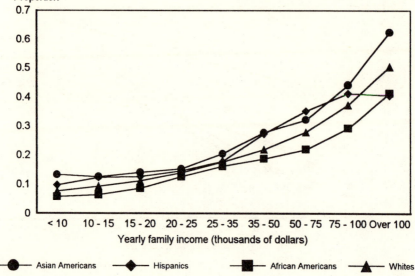

Parent Involvement in the Community

Coleman and Hoffer (1987) postulate that Catholic schools foster a sense of community among students, parents, and school personnel and that this adds to their success. A particularly important aspect of the community is its intergenerational nature, that parents know other parents and because they communicate they are better able to keep track of one another's children. Coleman (1988) refers to the kinds of networks that emerge when parents know the parents of their child's friends as having "intergenerational closure," and hypothesizes that these networks provide a foundation on which social norms become mutually understood and enforced. NELS:88 has information about whether the parent knows the parents of each of five friends of the student.[13] Figure 2.14 shows the average number of friends' parents known by the parents' educational level and by race/ethnicity.

Intergenerational closure is clearly characteristic of whites, and for each subgroup it is correlated with parent's level of education. As minority parents' level of education increases, they also know more parents, but they never come near the level of whites. White parents with a college degree or more know an average of 3.35 parents, whereas comparable figures for Asian Americans, Hispanics, and African Americans are 2.24, 2.65, and 2.50, respectively, each less than the mean for all whites (2.94), regardless

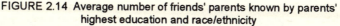

FIGURE 2.14 Average number of friends' parents known by parents'
highest education and race/ethnicity

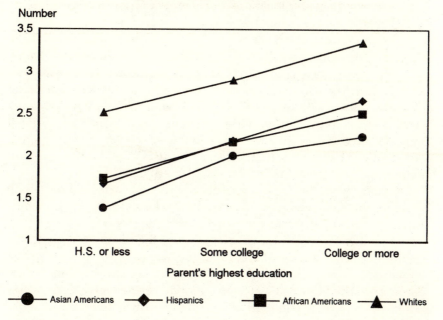

of education level. Insofar as the average number of parents known reflects the extent to which the child and parent share a common community, whites, and to some extent all parents with more education, have better access to this kind of community. The community may serve any number of functions, from establishing common norms among students to providing parents with networks to keep abreast of developments in school policy. It is likely to serve as reinforcement for parents and possibly a safety net of sorts.

Parent acquaintance networks are likely to be dependent on context in ways that are different from all the other forms of involvement. This is because access to parent networks depends upon the other parents who are available for acquaintance ties. Where parent participation in school activities may depend in part on qualities of the school (e.g., openness), access to acquaintance or friendship networks depends upon the composition of the community and the opportunity for interaction. Thus, similarities and differences in personal characteristics and activities of parents relative to the pool of potential acquaintances may be important. In this way, the racial/ethnic composition of the school might be a factor in parent friendships. This may explain why whites, who are most often the majority in a school, have higher rates of parent friendships.

Parent Involvement with the School

Parent involvement with the school may take a variety of forms. Parents might become involved to intervene in a problem, or they may be interested in program options which are available, in order to guide their child in making the best decision. They might want to have influence on school policy or may become involved as a way to form social relationships with other parents. Three forms of school involvement are considered here. First is parent contact with the school about academic matters concerning the child. It tends to be topic specific, focusing on the child's educational progress. Second is parent volunteer work at school. Third is parent participation in a parent-teacher organization (PTO). The last two forms of involvement are general rather than child specific

Contact About Academics. Parents might contact the school about academic matters for several reasons. If a child is experiencing academic difficulty, contact may take the form of crisis intervention, which represents an attempt to marshal the resources of the school to address the specific needs of the child at that moment. Alternatively, in the case of a student who is performing well, contact may be an attempt to enhance the learning of a child through acquiring information about advanced courses or influencing a programming decision. Although these two "motives" for contact are distinct at one level, they also have a clear affinity—the parent is intervening in an attempt to influence a specific school decision or action regarding the child.

Four questions in NELS:88 pertain directly to this form of involvement. Parents reported on the frequency of contacts they initiated with the school about their child's academic performance and about academic programs, and the frequency with which schools contacted them about the same topics. Overall, approximately 52.4% of the parents said they had contacted their child's school about his or her academic performance at least once since school opened. Fewer parents (34.8%) said they had contacted the school about their child's academic programs over the same period. Parents who reported that the school had contacted them at least once were comparable, 54.8% about academic performance and 35.3% about academic program. The principal focus here will be on parent initiated contact rather than school initiated contact, since the analytical emphasis is on parent action, and the former more directly measures this.

For analytic purposes, the two forms of parent initiated contact were summed, producing a constructed variable representing frequency of contacts.[14] The average amount that parents contacted their child's school varies somewhat depending on race/ethnicity, as shown in Figure 2.15.

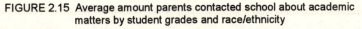

FIGURE 2.15 Average amount parents contacted school about academic matters by student grades and race/ethnicity

Frequency of times contacting school

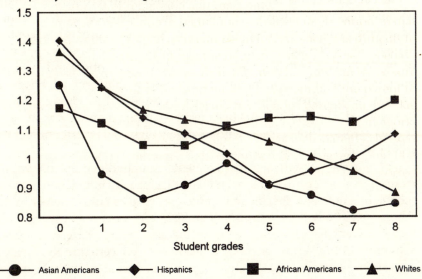

Student grades

● Asian Americans   ◆ Hispanics   ■ African Americans   ▲ Whites

Asian American parents are least likely to report contact overall: Only about 47% of Asian American parents report such contact as compared with more than one-half of Hispanic, African American, and white parents. African American parents (and Hispanic parents to a lesser extent) who contact the school do so at higher rates than their white counterparts. In addition, if these minority parents do contact the school they are more likely to do so multiple times.

Figure 2.15 also shows the relationship of contacts to student grades. In general, as the frequency of contact increases, student grades decrease. This relationship suggests that a strong element of "crisis intervention" is present in contact with the school. However, important differences emerge when the relationship between contact and grades is considered within racial groups. The negative relationship between grades and contacting about academic performance is most pronounced for whites. White parents whose children have very low grades (the bottom 10%) contact at an average of 1.37 times, while white parents with students who have grades in the top 10% contact .88 times, or about 60% less frequently. Thus, for white parents, the crisis intervention scenario seems plausible.

The relationship is quite different for African American parents. Among children in the lowest grade group, African American parents contact on average 1.17 times and, for children in the highest grade group, 1.20 times.

Their rate of contact stays nearly constant with respect to grades; it does not decrease significantly. Thus, while white and African American parents contact at comparable rates for low achieving children (this rate actually becomes higher for African Americans when differences in the parent's education are taken into account), African American parents also contact at high rates when their child is performing well. These parents appear to be incorporating both the elements of crisis intervention and positive intervention or enhancement into their contact with the school. Hispanic parents have a profile similar to African Americans although not as pronounced. The profile of Asian American parents shows lower levels of contact across all grade levels with relatively high contact rates only if the child exhibits extremely low grades.

Volunteering. As a form of involvement in the child's education, volunteering has a more diffuse character than other forms of interaction with the school. It is not child specific in that the parent does not volunteer in the school specifically to help his or her child, and it is not policy oriented in that the parent takes the role of assistant either in the classroom or in school activities. Volunteering is more indicative of concern for the overall educational experience of the child. It provides the parent with an opportunity to observe the working of the school as a type of participant/ observer. The influence of other students on the child's learning can be evaluated. The interaction of teachers with students can be viewed within the school context. And, by contributing to the school in this manner, the parent is in some way incorporated into the educational process within the school. It is important to note that this incorporation is directed in a significant part by the school staff and teachers. The role of volunteer is that of support, at least from the school's perspective.

Thus, the intention of this form of involvement is not likely to be direct intervention on behalf of the child. Nor is it necessarily an attempt to manage the child's educational experience or to bolster a child's poor academic performance. Rather, volunteering may be understood as engagement with the overall experience of the child's education through acquiring first-hand information about the environment of the school, interacting with teachers as they perform their jobs, and observing the interactions of the child with other students. Because volunteering is likely to take place during the time school is in session, parent participation will probably depend upon other commitments, like employment.

NELS:88 parents were asked if they had acted as a volunteer at the child's school during the year (they could respond yes or no). Figure 2.16 shows the responses by maternal employment status and race/ethnicity. Overall,

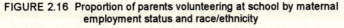

FIGURE 2.16 Proportion of parents volunteering at school by maternal
employment status and race/ethnicity

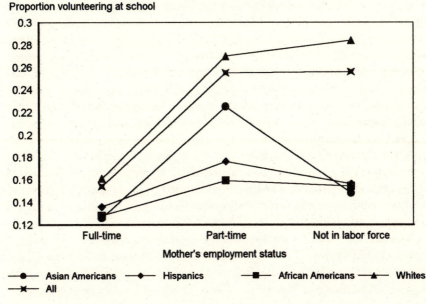

about 19% of the parents reported that they had volunteered. The main
constraint on volunteering seems to be maternal employment status;
mothers who work full-time volunteer at much lower rates. On average,
15.4% of the mothers who work full-time volunteer, in contrast to 24.3% and
26.0% of mothers who work part-time and are homemakers, respectively.

Participation in a Parent-Teacher Organization. The educational process takes place in the context of an organization, namely the school. Parents
may display involvement, not only directly through the child, but by
participating in the formal organization of the school through the PTO.
Questions of school policy may be dealt with, program options for students
may be discussed, extracurricular activities for students may be planned,
and allocation of school funds may be debated in PTO meetings. In general,
the PTO serves as a means of communication and involvement between the
school administration and parents. It may also provide an arena in which
social relationships among parents are fostered.

Parents were asked about three kinds of participation in PTO: belonging
to a PTO, attending PTO meetings, and taking part in PTO activities.
Approximately 31.9% of the parents stated that they belonged to the
organization, while 36.1% said they attended meetings. White parents tend
to report belonging at a higher rate, but African Americans report the

highest rate of attendance. However, when examined by parents' education level and race/ethnicity, this apparent anomaly disappears. When educational level is held constant, African Americans report belonging and attending at higher rates. "Membership," then, appears to be more a function of parent's education and probably social status. Attendance, although also influenced by social status, appears to be a more accessible activity. Consequently, after accounting for differences in educational level, African American parents display higher general rates of engagement with the PTO. This is true for Hispanics as well, although to a lesser extent. Asian Americans are involved at lower levels even after controlling for parents' educational level.

A variable may be constructed to capture the general level of involvement in the PTO, allowing general trends to be more easily evaluated.[15] When this constructed variable is evaluated with respect to parents' education and race/ethnicity, as shown in Figure 2.17, we observe a strong positive relationship for all racial/ethnic subgroups.

African American parents with a college degree or more participate at especially high rates.[16] The average increase for all parents is from .67 for parents without a high school degree to 1.47 for parents with the highest degree, an increase of more than 130%. The levels and rates of increase

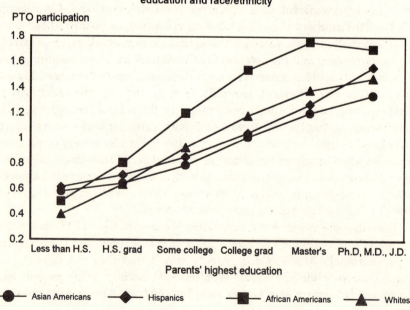

FIGURE 2.17 Average PTO participation by parents' highest education and race/ethnicity

among the whites, Hispanics, and Asian Americans are not appreciably different when parent's education level is controlled.

Summary

Our purpose in this chapter has been to describe some of the ways parents may become involved in their child's education. In doing so, patterns have emerged which have to do with similarities and differences in who becomes involved, especially racial and ethnic differences, and in some of the conditions of involvement. We will briefly review these patterns.

Racial and Ethnic Differences in Parent Involvement. We have seen that whites have especially high levels of involvement only in areas for which there is a major component related to social activities and a view of education as a form of cultural enrichment: talking about current school experiences, knowing the parents of their child's friends, and volunteering at school. Asian Americans provide an interesting contrast to the other groups. In many areas they exhibit low levels of involvement. In the home they show lowest levels of talk between parents and child about high school program planning. They tend not to know other parents or become involved with the school. However, they are highest in restrictions on television and highest in enrolling their child in extra classes. They also tend to save more money for college and spend more on education. Asian American involvement appears to be sparsest on activities in which social interaction is a significant component.[17]

Like Asian American involvement, African American involvement is directed in nature, but differs from the other racial and ethnic groups in several respects. Mothers talk with their child about high school program planning, participate in PTO, and enroll their child in computer classes at high rates. African Americans, unlike other groups, appear to engage in "crisis intervention" activity at higher rates than others, as demonstrated by their high levels of checking homework and contacting the school about academic matters. This may be a stylistic difference or may be because the children have more problems that demand intervention.

Hispanic parents also present a different pattern of involvement. They tend to spend more on current educational expenses in comparison to other groups and are more likely to restrict television viewing than whites and African Americans.

Differences in Forms of Involvement. No two forms of the involvement selected have the same qualities. Of the more than 160 measures of parent involvement in NELS:88, we have selected a small sample.[18] If one refers back to the process discussed in the introduction, the purpose of this chapter has been to open up the black box of "parent involvement" in an effort to understand the texture and substance of different parent actions. The forms of involvement selected should each have a unique set of parameters associated with the combination of resources, motivation, and context. They are likely also to have differential influence on the academic behavior of students.

There are two main themes which run throughout the types of parent involvement. One has to do with the context in which the actions take place. Context is an important issue for several reasons. A context other than the home is subject to additional constraints related to characteristics of that context. Home-based involvement, while subject to resource constraints like family income or parents' education, may be more stable over time, since the constraints are least likely to involve other actors. For this reason, home-based involvement may most accurately reflect a historical component of the parents' involvement in the child's education.

The second theme has to do with the motivation of the parent for action. Some actions of parents appear to be instrumental in nature, designed to have a directed impact, while others are actions in which parents seem to engage as a matter of course. Some instrumental action has an intervention quality, possibly designed to avert a negative consequence. Parents appear to use homework checking and contacting the school as vehicles of this kind of intervention. Other instrumental action may be designed to make optimal use of available resources. This type of action is more difficult to distinguish from activities performed as a matter of course, but it stands to reason that an activity like PTO participation is often instrumental. For example, parents may attend meetings to acquire useful information to help the child or facilitate decision making (e.g., program decisions) or to try to influence a school policy. Ties outside the family may also include an affective component, and parents may engage in them as a matter of course, although ties to the school are likely to have a direct, purposive component. We should remember that such relationships are subject to the constraints of other actors.

When parents are involved in a more affective way, the motivation may be related to a desire for the child to do well in school, but the action tends not to be targeted at influencing a particular event. The way parents structure the home environment, both through conversation and rules, is an example of this more general involvement, as is providing the child with extra music classes. But even when a direct consequence is not intended, the action may have a significant impact on the child's experiences.

Thus, there appear to be two important dimensions related to context and motivation. Our understanding of involvement can be enhanced when these dimensions are considered, because they provide information about the constraints on involvement and about the circumstances and possible history of the parent action. When context involves other actors, as involvement in the school or community does, then it is subject to constraints of that context. As a matter of course, actions taken by parents reflecting underlying values, priorities, and styles, are least likely to be subject to change. The same may be said of actions which are least subject to external constraints, such as many activities that take place in the home. The actions of parents which involve their child and their child's education most probably come about from a balance of parent interests and family resources. The combination of the two factors will make a difference in the opportunity structure of parents and the decisions they make about taking advantage of opportunities for the child during the educational process.

Notes

1. Appendix 2.1 contains details on all constructed variables presented in this chapter.

2. The variable "talk about current school experiences" ranges in value from zero (which represents a response of "never") to two (which represents a response of "three or more times").

3. As is the case with the previous variable, a response of zero means that the student and parent never talk and a response of two indicates the student and parent have talked "three or more times during the school year."

4. The grade categories shown have approximately the same number of students in each group.

5. The moving average is calculated by averaging an observation (in this case the mean level of talking) with the observation in the previous category of student grades. The observations for the first and last categories of student grades are not averages of two categories, rather they are simply the average level of talking for students of the lowest and highest grade category. The graphs in which data have been smoothed that follow have been subjected to the same technique for smoothing.

6. Studies of parent involvement and home environment of preschool children point to the importance of both the amount and the quality of verbal interaction for the child's early measures of achievement. Parent involvement in the form of talking, especially about current school experiences, is no doubt measuring some of the same basic elements of the parent-child relationship but at different stages of the child's development.

7. The interaction between regulation and discussion has to do with Baumrind's types of parenting style. She identifies three types: authoritative, authoritarian, and permissive.

8. In the case of both homework checking and restricting television, possible responses range from one, which represents a student response that the parent "never" engages in the regulatory action, to four, which represents a response of

"often." The other two categories are "rarely" and "sometimes," thus an average level of restriction of 3.5 would represent an average response midway between the categories "often" and "sometimes."

9. Fehrmann, Keith, and Reimers (1987) studied amount of television watched and student grades using seniors in the base year of High School and Beyond. They found that time spent on homework leads to higher student grades, and they found that students who watched less television got slightly higher grades.

10. Figure 2.9 originally appeared in Muller, Schiller, and Lee (1991). We thank Kathryn Schiller and Seh-Ahn Lee for allowing this to be included here.

11. Part of the difference in level of after school supervision between part-time and full-time employees could be because mothers who work part-time may be employed in closer proximity to the home. The data do not allow us to consider if this is the case.

12. Single mothers who are not in the labor force are a small and diverse group. Without further analysis it would be difficult to draw any conclusions about them.

13. Friends are named by the student, and not all students name five friends. The variable constructed here is simply a summation of the number of friends' parents known.

14. The variables used for this construct range in value from one to three. Exploratory analysis indicated that the two highest categories should be collapsed into one. In addition, each variable was rescaled so that zero represents no contact.

15. The exact construction of the variable may be found in the Appendix 2.1.

16. Even when parents' education is not controlled, however, the difference in participation rates of African Americans and others is marked, 1.01 versus .94, .91, and .79 for whites, Asian Americans, and Hispanics, respectively.

17. This may be related to the fact that Asian Americans are rarely in a racial majority. In many Asian cultures, in China, Japan, and Korea, for example, involvement of parents in schools is widespread and encouraged, but, there Asian parents are in a racial majority.

18. Selection of forms of involvement was based on an effort to obtain variables that at once measured different dimensions of involvement and appeared to be valid measures of the stated activity.

Appendix 2.1

Description of Constructed Variables

Maternal employment status. Parent response about the employment status of the mother. Responses of working full-time, part-time, and not in labor force were used. Parents with other responses are excluded from analysis.

Talk about current school experiences. Constructed from student responses to the questions, "Since the beginning of the school year, how often have you discussed the following with either or both of your parents or guardians?" (1) "school activities" and (2) "things you've studied in class." Responses were summed to range from 0 to 4 and divided by two, thus the variable construct ranges from 0 to 2. The category for a single variable with the value of 0 represents a response category of "not at all" and 2 represents "three or more times."

Talk about high school program. Constructed from student responses about the frequency with which the student has talked with the (1) father or (2) mother "about planning your high school program." If the student response to the question of talking with the father was greater than 0, then the value for that response was used. Otherwise the response for talking with the mother was used. The range is 0 to 2, with 0="not at all" and 2="three or more times."

Friends' parents known. Summation of the parents of the child's friends known. Parents were first asked to identify the first names of up to five of the child's friends. Then parents were asked "whether you know the parents of that child." The variable was coded "yes"=1, "no"=0. Responses were summed to range from 0 to 5.

Frequency parents contact school. Constructed from parent responses to two questions, "Since your eighth grader's school opened last fall, how many times have you or your spouse/partner contacted the school about each of the following:" (1) "Your eighth grader's academic performance?" and (2) "Your eighth grader's academic program for this year?" Two response categories, "three or four times" and "more than four times," are combined and the variables rescaled to range from 0 to 2 where 0=none. The two responses are then summed to produce a variable ranging from 0 to 4.

PTO participation. Constructed from parent responses to the questions, "Do you and your spouse/partner do any of the following at your eighth grader's school?" (1) "Belong to a parent-teacher organization"; (2) "Attend meetings of a parent-teacher organization"; and (3) "Take part in the activities of a parent-teacher organization." Responses were 1=yes, 0=no, and summed for a variable ranging from 0 to 3.

Student grades. Students in NELS:88 were asked to report their grades "from sixth grade up till now" in four subject areas (English, mathematics, science, and social studies). From these self-reports, The National Center for Education Statistics (NCES) constructed a composite average in which all subjects are weighted equally to produce a variable ranging from .5 to 4.0 (a student report that grades for a subject are "mostly below D's" was assigned a value of .5). For the figures presented in this chapter, this variable was then divided into nine categories with approximately the equal number of students.

3

Family Structure Effects on Student Outcomes

Seh-Ahn Lee

The changing dynamics of two societal institutions, the family and the school, have drawn the attention of many scholars, policy makers, and lay persons in American society. Within the family, rising rates of divorce and separation and increasing numbers of out-of-wedlock births are leading social researchers to regard single parent families as no longer "atypical" (Epstein 1990; Garfinkel and McLanahan 1986). About 50% of all children born in the 1980s will live with only one parent for at least 3 years before reaching age 18 (Astone and McLanahan 1991; Sweet and Bumpass 1987).

The rise in the number of single parent families has created yet another phenomenon. It is now quite common for a child to experience diverse family situations: at one point in time the child may live with his or her natural mother only; at another point the mother might marry and then the child would be living in a melded family. It has been found that many formerly married mothers remarry and that, among children whose mothers remarry, about one-half experience a second family disruption before age 16 (Garfinkel and McLanahan 1986; Sweet and Bumpass 1987).

Studies that highlight the multiple family disruptions experienced by children provide at least two insights into the analysis of family structure. First, as Bumpass (1984) contends, figures obtained from any cross-sectional data grossly underestimate the number of children spending some portions of their lives in single parent families, particularly households headed by single mothers. This underestimation occurs because remarriages of mothers lead to a much smaller number of children living in single parent families at any point in time than living in single parent families sometime during their childhood. In addition, we should note that many children found in single parent families at one time will have already experienced or will later experience living in other types of families, e.g., stepparent families.

Since approximately one-half of remarriages will end in divorce before a child in the family has reached the age of 16, the available cross-sectional data do not allow examination of the full effects of single parent families. We can only suggest that any observed effects of the child's current family structure are not solely the result of the current structure, but include the effects of prior structures, due to the transitory nature of the modern American family.

These changes in the family have consequences for children's education. Today schools are criticized for the low levels of student performance. This issue is so urgent that the President and the Governors established six "highly ambitious" goals for the educational system. They state:

> . . . the time has come, for the first time in U.S. history, to establish clear national performance goals, goals that will make us internationally competitive.[1]

These goals, which require "sweeping and fundamental" changes in the American educational system, underscore the seriousness of the problems in American education. During the past two or three decades, research has shown an association between student outcomes and the deteriorating educational climate of American elementary and/or high schools (Coleman 1987; Diprete 1981). One factor contributing heavily to this deterioration of educational climate is change in the family.

Recognizing that changes in the school's functioning may result from changes in the family, this chapter asks: (1) How does family structure impact student educational outcomes, e.g., standardized test scores in reading and mathematics, grades, and misbehavior? and (2) How does parental involvement affect student outcomes within each family structure? Many studies have been very successful in drawing attention to these issues, but the focus has been mainly on small segments of the student population, such as poor African American students living with single mothers (Dornbusch et al. 1985; Dornbusch et al. 1987; Milne et al. 1986; Shinn 1978). The pattern of family disorganization is not confined to a certain racial or ethnic group, or certain social strata; the proportion of students experiencing family disorganization is rapidly increasing in all segments of the population.

This analysis focuses on differences in parental involvement in the household, along with other student demographic background characteristics, individual psychological state, and the socio-economic status of the family. In other words, we take up the question, with some assumptions, of how strongly or weakly three student outcomes are related to such characteristics as socio-economic status, the measurements of parental involvement in the family, students' psychological well-being, gender, and race and ethnicity within each type of family.[2]

First, we examine the direct influence of exogenous background variables (parent education, students' gender, and race), family structure, and intervening variables of family functioning on the three student outcome variables: standardized test scores, grades, and misbehavior. Second, the background variables and family structure are assumed also to have indirect effects on students' educational outcomes through intervening variables. Thus, the intervening variables—parental involvement in the context of the family, family income, and students' psychological well-being—are considered first to be affected by the background characteristics and family structure, and second to influence student outcomes. The relationships to be examined are expressed in Figure 3.1.

Two broadly defined types of family structure—a traditional family where a student is living with his or her biological mother and father and a non-traditional family where a student is living with a single parent, in a melded family, or with relatives or guardians—are the points of focus. If there is a negative effect of non-traditional family structure, we expect that when there are no statistical controls the outcome measures for children from traditional families will be higher (i.e., better grades and test scores, etc.) than those for children from non-traditional families. Further, non-

FIGURE 3.1 Relationship between background, intervening, and dependent variables

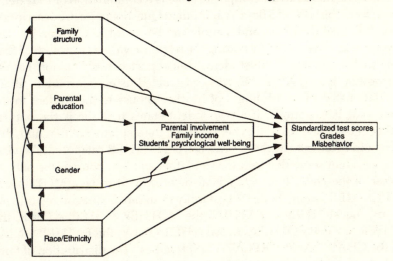

traditional families can be expected to be less involved with their students' education as compared to traditional families. The intervening variables of family functioning, that is, lack of parental involvement, family income, and students' individual psychological well-being, are expected to impact the educational outcomes of students negatively. This chapter has four sections. The first section describes the variables used in the analysis. The second section highlights the differences in the average of each outcome measure among the various family types, allowing us to compare the average outcomes in traditional families with those in non-traditional families. The third section investigates the relationship between the outcome variables and family structure, with other background characteristics being controlled in the analysis. The background variables considered at this stage are distinguished from the intervening variables in that the former (parent education, gender, and race/ethnicity) are assumed not to be affected by family structure. The fourth section discusses the intervening variables both as factors affecting student outcomes and as variables affected by the background variables and by family structure. (For related works, see Baker and Stevenson 1986; Clifton 1986; Dornbusch et al. 1985; Milne et al. 1986; Shinn 1978.)

Dependent, Intervening, and Background Variables

Table 3.A.1 (Appendix 3.1) provides a description of the variables and their sources. The dependent variables are standardized test scores composite for reading and math, grades composite, and a misbehavior composite scale. The misbehavior composite scale is a combination of four items chosen from the NELS:88 Base Year Student Questionnaire. (A description of the NELS:88 data base and sample can be found in Chapter 1.) The measure was constructed by adding the response values from each of four items that asked about the students' self-reported misbehavior. Family composition type (FAMTYPE) was constructed using information about the relationship of an adult and of his/her spouse to the student in the household. For example, if a respondent states that she is the natural mother of the student and that her spouse is the stepfather of the child, this household belongs to the MOTHER & STEPFATHER category. Likewise, if a respondent states that he is the stepfather and his spouse is the natural mother of the child, this family is also considered to be a MOTHER & STEPFATHER family. In this way, family structure is categorized into six groups, the MOTHER & FATHER, the MOTHER & STEPFATHER, the FATHER & STEPMOTHER, the MOTHER ONLY, the FATHER ONLY, and the GUARDIAN(S)/RELATIVE(S) families.[3] The distribution of family types across the whole sample is presented in Table 3.1.[4]

TABLE 3.1 Categorization and distribution of family structure

Family structure	N	Percent(%)
Mother and Father	14,476	65.3
Mother and Stepfather	2,386	10.8
Father and Stepmother	588	2.7
Mother only	3,735	16.9
Father only	461	2.1
Guardian(s)/Relative(s)	508	2.3
Total	22,154	100

The exogenous background characteristics used in this analysis include parental education (PA_EDUC), the student's gender (SEX), and race/ethnicity (RACE). PA_EDUC is the higher of the two educational levels of the father or mother or guardian/relative in two-adult families, and the mother's educational level or father's educational level for single parent families. SEX is female and male, while RACE is categorized into four racial/ethnic groups: whites, African Americans, Hispanics, and Asian Americans.[5]

The four intervening variables include two measures of parental involvement, namely, "inter-generational closure" (INGECL) (Coleman and Hoffer 1987) and the frequency of students discussing school matters with parents (DISCUSS); family income (FINCOME); and students' psychological well-being (SATISFY). INGECL is based on the parent's report of the number of parents of the child's friends the parent knows (minimum is 0, maximum is 5). This concept of "inter-generational closure" is used for its importance in fostering networks of a community that provide a means by which parents can monitor their children through social norms mutually understood and enforced (Coleman 1988).

DISCUSS was constructed by summing up the responses to three items listed in Table 3.A.1 in the same manner as for the misbehavior scale.[6] FINCOME was derived by using the mid-point value for the range included in a family's income category, as presented in the questionnaire. When this variable was used in an ordinary least squares (OLS) regression, logged income was taken for the estimation of parameters. Finally, a measure of the student's psychological well-being was constructed by combining two measures of self-consciousness about his/her importance in the student body (BYS56C and BYS56D in Table 3.A.1) and on the basis of the student's overall satisfaction measure (BYS44H). That is, students were first ordered by their degree of overall satisfaction, and then within each group of students showing the same degree of overall satisfaction, by their self-reports of how other students viewed them.

Zero-order Relationship Between Family Structure and Student Outcomes

To get both an idea about the effect of family structure on student outcomes and an accurate sense about family structures as they exist in American society, it is useful to examine the zero-order relationship between family structure and student outcomes. Thus, the first task is to investigate whether there is any significant difference in student outcomes among different types of families without using statistical controls.

Achievement Measured by Standardized Test Scores. Table 3.2 presents the means and their confidence intervals for each student outcome measure. As has been shown in other research, students from traditional families show the highest average standardized test scores.[7] Among non-traditional families, families headed by guardians have the lowest average student test scores followed by mother only families. Reconstituted families with either a stepmother or a stepfather and father only families have similar averages, which are higher than mother only and guardian headed families. The average score for guardian headed families is about 70% of a standard deviation of the total sample below that for mother-father families; and for mother only families, the average score is about 40% below mother-father families; for father only and melded families, the average score is about 25% below mother-father families.

From these comparisons, at least three inferences may be drawn as preliminary findings: (1) The average student in traditional families scores well above the average student in any non-traditional family. (2) Students in families with at least one natural parent have average test scores much higher than those of students in guardian headed families. (3) Excluding guardian headed families, single mother families have the lowest average score compared to other types of families.

TABLE 3.2 Means of outcome variables within each type of family

Variables		Family structure					
	Total	M&F	M&SF	F&SM	MO	FO	G/R
Test scores	50.46	51.65	49.29	49.15	47.75	49.02	44.78
c.i.'s	50.33,50.59	51.49,51.81	48.91,49.67	48.42,49.88	47.43,48.07	48.08,49.96	44.00,45.56
Grades	2.91	3.00	2.78	2.72	2.71	2.74	2.62
c.i.'s	2.90,2.92	2.99,3.01	2.75,2.81	2.66,2.78	2.69,2.74	2.67,2.81	2.56,2.68
Misbehavior	5.08	4.91	5.30	5.58	5.41	5.41	5.72
c.i.'s	5.06,5.10	4.89,4.94	5.23,5.37	5.43,5.73	5.35,5.47	5.23,5.59	5.54,5.90

Note: Standard deviations of variables within each type of family structure are presented in Appendix 3.1, Table 3.A.2. "c.i." refers to a confidence interval of the mean.

Achievement Measured by Grades. As in standardized test scores, the family with both natural parents is the highest on the average of the grades composite, followed by the mother & stepfather family, the father only family, the father & stepmother family, the mother only family, and the guardian headed family in descending order. Again, students from traditional families are higher than those from any other family group, while students in guardian headed families are the lowest. Observing the differences between traditional families and other groups by a standard deviation of the total sample, mother-stepfather and father only families are about one-third of a standard deviation below mother-father families; father-stepmother and mother only families are about two-fifths below; and guardian headed families one-half below. Although there is a slight inconsistency in the order of family types with respect to average grades composite and average standardized test scores, we still do find significant differences between traditional and non-traditional families.

Student Misbehavior. Children from traditional families have the lowest level of misbehavior while those from guardian headed families have the highest mean value. Rearranging the means from the different family types in ascending order,[8] the mother & stepfather family is about a quarter of a standard deviation above the mother & father family; the mother only family and the father only family are a little less than one-third above the mother & father family; the father & stepmother family is about two-fifths above the mother & father family; and the guardian headed family is about one-half above the mother & father family.

These results for standardized test scores, grades, and misbehavior provide some general but very preliminary findings. Not all types of non-traditional two-parent families have students who on average perform or behave better than those in single parent (either a father or a mother) families. It appears that the average student in father only families is either the same or better than the average student in families with a father and a stepmother for the overall outcome measures. The implication of this finding is that student outcomes are affected by factors other than the number of parents.[9] It also appears that, regarding all three outcome variables, the family headed by guardians or relatives is the most undesirable family structure.

Effects of Family Structure on Student Outcomes with Background Characteristics Taken into Account

The early research literature on the effect of family structure on student outcomes has often been criticized for its failure to control for family background characteristics other than family structure. It has been clearly shown that many aspects of family backgrounds, or environments, are related to school achievement (Baker and Stevenson 1986; Clifton et al. 1986; Coleman 1988; Jencks et al. 1972; Majoribanks 1979; Moles 1992; Pallas et al. 1989; Rumberger et al. 1990; Shinn 1978). As Coleman (1988) argues, "family background" has been considered a single entity in many studies on achievement in school. There is no single "family background." Accepting Coleman's analytical separation, family background is viewed from at least three different dimensions: parent education, family income, and parent involvement with one's children in their education within the family context, aside from the ascriptive characteristics of the students. Theoretically, we can conceptualize parental involvement in children's education as "social capital" in the home context. In the same vein, family income is termed as "financial capital" in the family, and parent education as "human capital" in the family.

Explanations for how and why background variables are related to school achievement are necessary when investigating the effect of family structure. First, parent education is considered to be an especially important factor in the educational environment for children. Many studies show that children of poorly educated parents are lower achievers in school than those of better educated parents. One explanation of this might be that better educated parents have more knowledge of their children's schooling, are more likely to be involved in the instructional process in school, and have higher academic expectations for their children (Baker and Stevenson 1986).

Second, racial or ethnic status and gender are also well-established indicators of students' performance. Many studies have been done which attempt to uncover the sources of the educational disadvantages faced by African-Americans and Hispanics. One explanation is that their economic position is well below the poverty line; in other words, there is socioeconomic deprivation. Another explanation involves the whole educational process, including the interaction of teachers with students. After examining teachers' expectations of students from six racial/ethnic groups, Clifton et al. (1986) conclude that students' ethnicity and gender have an effect on their teachers' expectations, which suggests that students' ascribed characteristics are actually used in teachers' evaluations of students. If this is true, these evaluations will affect students' performance at school.[10]

Do family structural effects on student outcomes remain for students with backgrounds that are otherwise comparable? This section is designed to begin to answer this question which must be confronted in order to understand the function of the family through its structure.[11]

TABLE 3.3 Distribution of PA_EDUC, SEX, and RACE by family structure

Variables		Total	M&F	M&SF	F&SM	MO	FO	G/R
PA_EDUC	High school or less	42.4	37.7	44.4	45.4	56.3	45.7	61.3
	College or more	57.6	62.3	55.6	54.6	43.7	54.3	38.7
SEX	Male	50.0	50.3	47.5	57.9	48.2	57.3	51.5
	Female	50.0	49.7	52.5	42.1	51.8	42.7	48.5
RACE	Asian Americans	3.4	4.1	1.6	2.0	1.5	5.1	3.7
	Hispanics	9.6	9.7	8.8	7.5	10.2	8.0	9.8
	African Americans	12.6	7.5	12.1	7.8	30.6	9.6	37.4
	Whites	74.4	78.7	77.5	82.8	57.6	77.3	49.2

Note: Column total for each variable is 100%.

Table 3.3 presents the distribution of PA_EDUC, RACE, and SEX by each type of family structure. Particularly noticeable in this table is the variation in the distribution of the racial/ethnic background and of the parental education. For example, African Americans are highly underrepresented in families with both natural parents as well as in families reconstituted with a father and stepmother, and they are highly overrepresented in both guardian headed and single mother families. In fact, African Americans are more likely to be in either guardian headed or single mother families than any other type of family. This may be primarily due to the high rate of out-of-wedlock births concentrated in African American families and to the growth in the population of never-married mothers (Garfinkel and McLanahan 1986).

Meanwhile, Asian Americans are very much underrepresented in the categories of mother-stepfather families, father-stepmother families and mother only families. In father only families, however, Asian Americans are overrepresented by about 50% (p value is less than .01). Results for Asian Americans contrast sharply with those found for African-Americans. It seems that, unlike African Americans, Asian American 8th graders are likely to be in father only families or father-stepmother families in the case of a family disruption. Such a disruption, however, is relatively unlikely for Asian American families. With regard to parent education, parent education of high school or less is overrepresented in guardian headed families and mother only families.

Thus, the background characteristics of race/ethnicity, gender, and parents' education were used as controls in the regression analysis to account for the differences among family structure in three student outcomes and to calculate the estimated mean value of each student outcome within each type of family structure. The three outcomes were regressed separately within each type of family on the background variables to allow for the different effects of background characteristics in different family types. After the separate regression analysis for each outcome, the estimated difference between non-traditional and traditional families was calculated by first obtaining the predicted average outcome measures within each type of family for a student with background characteristics standardized to those of the average student in the total sample, and then by finding the increment or decrement for each type of family.[12]

Standardized Test Scores. The negative differences in the second line of Table 3.4 for each type of non-traditional family show that, controlling for background characteristics, students in these family types generally have lower achievement than those in mother-father families. This association between family structure and student achievement level is consistent with the previous findings from the zero-order relationship. However, the differences are reduced compared to the raw differences presented in the first line of Table 3.4. Comparing the background-controlled differences (i.e., a total effect of family structure) of non-traditional families with one another, we find a dramatic reduction of the difference in mother only families, in which almost 75% of the raw differences are eliminated by controlling background variables. For other types of non-traditional families, about 40% of the raw differences are removed except in father-stepmother families, where only 22% are removed. This reduction of the raw differences can be attributed to the fact that the backgrounds of non-traditional families are very different from those of traditional families.

On the basis of this comparison, it is possible to draw some inferences: (1) In general, there is still evidence that traditional families perform better than non-traditional families with respect to the student outcomes mea-

TABLE 3.4 Total effect of family structure estimated by differences of outcomes between traditional families and each type of non-traditional family with PA_EDUC, SEX, and RACE standardized

| Outcome variables | M&F | Family structure | | | | |
		M&SF	F&SM	MO	FO	G/R
Test scores						
Raw differences	--	-2.36(.21)	-2.50(.39)	-3.90(.18)	-2.63(.49)	-6.78(.41)
Total effect	--	-1.37	-1.95	-.97	-1.64	-4.29
Grades						
Raw differences	--	-.22(.02)	-.28(.03)	-.29(.01)	-.26(.04)	-.38(.03)
Total effect	--	-.19	-.18	-.11	-.21	-.28
Misbehavior						
Raw differences	--	.39(.04)	.67(.08)	.50(.03)	.50(.09)	.81(.09)
Total effect	--	.42	.58	.32	.34	.82

Note: Raw differences can be calculated directly from the average values of students' outcomes shown in Table 3.2. Standard errors of raw differences are in parentheses.

sured by standardized test scores. (2) Among non-traditional families, students in mother only families perform at the highest level, followed by those in mother-stepfather, father only, father-stepmother, and guardian headed families, in descending order.[13] Unlike the results in Table 3.2, we now see a reduced difference (about 10% of one standard deviation) in the standardized test scores between mother-father families and mother only families. Taking into account this fact, it might be said that the low achievement of students in the mother only category is largely due to their disadvantaged background compared to that of their counterparts in other family types.[14] One consistent finding is that students in guardian headed families, on average, perform at the lowest level. Interestingly, father-stepmother families seem worse than any other type of family structure, except guardian headed families. Of the two melded family types, mother-stepfather and father-stepmother families, the latter appear to be less functional in students' achievement on the standardized test scores than the former.

Grades. As for standardized test scores, the differences between students from traditional families and non-traditional families in grades are reduced greatly by statistically controlling on parents' education, gender, and race or ethnicity (shown in the third line of Table 3.4), except in mother-stepfather and father only families. Leaving aside guardian headed families, which seem to consistently have the most negative effect on grades, father only, mother-stepfather, and father-stepmother families are lower than mother only families. Particularly, for mother-stepfather and father only families, less than one-fifth of the raw difference is reduced, holding other background characteristics constant. This small proportion of change in mother-stepfather families and in father only families can be due to either or both of two factors. First, the background characteristics of students in these family types are not very different from those in mother-father families. Second, the background characteristics have little impact on students' grades. In the same vein, the 62% reduction in mother only families seems to suggest that low grades of students in this family type may be due to disadvantaged backgrounds, such as lower incomes and lower parent education levels combined with a strong effect of these background factors (see Table 3.A.6).

Misbehavior. The sixth line of Table 3.4 shows the estimated differences for the misbehavior measure. The negligible change from the raw differences (shown in the fifth line) for mother-stepfather families and guardian headed families shows that the high level of students' misbehavior in these family types, as compared to the level of students in mother-father families, remains unchanged even when holding the background characteristics constant. For the remaining categories, raw differences are reduced about 15% to 35% after standardization of the backgrounds, implying that the background differences in these types of families partially account for the greater levels of misbehavior. Across each type of non-traditional family, the overall standardized measures of the average student's misbehavior are consistently shown to be higher than the estimation for traditional families.

Comparing the increments in each type of family structure, families headed by guardians again show the highest level of the average student's misbehavior. Thus, we can see that the students in this family type perform worst in all three areas of student outcomes, even after controlling or standardizing on student backgrounds. This chapter does not attempt to discover all possible factors affecting the low level of students' outcomes, particularly in guardian headed families, but it would not be implausible to infer that the family headed by guardians is the most ineffective family type in terms of the production of good student outcomes. Father-step-mother and mother-stepfather families are shown to be less effective than single mother and single father families, leading to the preliminary conclusion that families with any stepparents are less effective than families with a natural parent and no stepparents are more effective in inhibiting student misbehavior than families with any stepparent.

Parental Involvement as Intervening Variables Between Family Structure and Student Outcomes

In the preceding sections, we demonstrated lower levels of educational outcomes in non-traditional families than in traditional families. Across all three areas of outcome measures, students in traditional families are seen to be consistently higher than those in other types of families in the level of academic performance, and lower in the level of misbehavior. This result holds whether background characteristics are controlled or not, supporting strongly the hypotheses that students in traditional families are better situated than students in non-traditional families regarding their educational outcomes and that there is variation in functional efficiency among different types of families. These findings, then, lead us to raise the question of why some family types produce better student outcomes than others. This inquiry is closely related to our concern that the proportion of children from educationally disadvantaged backgrounds is increasing in the school and in society at large. Clearly, this is of great significance to educational policy issues concerning students' outcomes in schools as well as to public policy issues concerning trends in family disorganization. This question is dealt with in this section by analyzing the effects of family characteristics related to family structure which may have direct impact on student outcomes.

The strategy for the analysis is as follows: Within each type of family, the relations of the four intervening variables with family structure and with each student outcome are examined through multivariate regression and standardization in order to find how much of the differences in student outcomes among different types of family structure can be accounted for by these intervening variables. The four intervening variables are two forms of parental involvement in the context of the family, family income, and students' overall feeling about psychological well-being. As mentioned earlier, student outcomes are assumed to be influenced not only by students' backgrounds, such as PA_EDUC, RACE, and SEX, and by a family structural type, but also by some factors which are thought to be dependent upon family structure. Of these factors, the two variables of social capital in the family, DISCUSS and INGECL (see Table 3.A.1) are the focus of discussion in this section. The former can be understood as the strength of parental involvement with their children in matters of schooling and the latter as the degree of communication among parents of different children.[15]

As in the previous section, a separate regression analysis was carried out with each outcome measure as a dependent variable within each type of family structure, using the same background characteristics as before, as well as the two forms of parental involvement, family income, and students' psychological satisfaction. Two objectives are established in doing so. First, holding other individual and family background characteristics constant, we can see a direct effect of parental involvement on each student outcome. Second, holding the two forms of parental involvement constant also, we can calculate the estimated mean difference of outcomes after standardizing all the control variables within each type of family structure to the means of the total sample, that is, the direct effect of family structure on outcome, apart from effects due to parent involvement. Thus, an explanation can be suggested as to how the family structural effect on student outcomes operates through parental involvement.

Parental Involvement as Social Capital and Its Impact on Student Outcomes

As shown in Tables 3.5 through 3.7, results from the regression of the three student outcomes on both forms of parental involvement within each type of family are highly consistent in showing the coefficients of the parental involvement variables to be in the expected direction. It is by this fact that we are led to investigate further the effect of family structure on parental involvement. The hypothesis is that the lesser effectiveness of non-traditional families is in part due to their lower parental involvement in their children's education (Seeley 1989). Parental involvement with their children or with other parents is of course not the only means by which parents affect educational outcomes. However, parental involvement plays a role in a child's education, and it is connected most to the structure of the family, i.e., the formalized relations between parents and children. It is within this context that parental involvement is viewed as social capital to be used as a resource for education. The comparison of the coefficients of the two forms of parental involvement for each area of student outcome indicates that DISCUSS has more impact on outcome variables than INGECL. This fact, however, should be accepted tentatively in that the measure of each form of parental involvement is not exhaustive.

Direct and Indirect Effects of Family Structure on Student Outcomes

As mentioned earlier, there is another way of examining the effect of parental involvement on student outcomes. One can estimate the predicted mean value of each student outcome standardized to the student with the average backgrounds including the two forms of parental involvement and the two remaining intervening variables (i.e., FINCOME and SATISFY). The differences in each student outcome for each family structure with all predictor variables standardized are estimated and presented in the

TABLE 3.5 Parameter estimates for separate models relating background variables and other intervening variables to test scores within each family structure

Variables	M&F Coeff.	T	M&SF Coeff.	T	F&SM Coeff.	T	MO Coeff.	T	FO Coeff.	T	G/R Coeff.	T
PA_EDUC	1.15	26.55**	.95	8.44**	.99	4.47**	.72	8.28**	.65	2.67**	.32	1.19
SEX	-.93	-5.86**	.04	.09	-.29	-.37	-.70	-2.26*	-1.75	-1.73	-.28	-.28
ASIAN	1.17	2.89**	-.47	-.29	-1.70	-.60	-2.01	-1.61	.48	.22	.42	.15
HISPANIC	-3.00	-10.79**	-2.68	-3.73**	-5.24	-3.52**	-4.03	-7.53**	-3.96	-2.15*	-3.78	-2.13*
BLACK	-6.09	-19.99**	-4.49	-6.98**	-6.00	-4.08**	-6.60	-18.35**	-7.17	-4.12**	-4.26	-3.74**
INGECL	.33	6.46**	.52	3.95**	-.39	-1.58	.38	3.92**	.10	.33	.45	1.50
DISCUSS	1.28	22.47**	1.20	8.50**	.99	3.62**	1.17	11.27**	1.20	3.65**	.73	2.26*
FINCOME	1.31	13.35**	1.31	5.31**	1.93	3.34**	.92	7.38**	1.25	2.04*	.87	2.10*
SATISFY	.20	11.28**	.03	.73	.26	3.03**	.10	3.14**	.02	.22	.03	.34
Intercept	9.75	9.78**	13.81	5.52**	6.62	1.13	22.16	14.59**	20.90	3.40**	28.32	5.26**
R²	.27		.20		.21		.25		.19		.13	

* = significant at .05 level; ** = significant at .01 level

TABLE 3.6 Parameter estimates for separate models relating background variables and other intervening variables to grades within each family structure

Variables	M&F Coeff.	T	M&SF Coeff.	T	F&SM Coeff.	T	MO Coeff.	T	FO Coeff.	T	G/R Coeff.	T
PA_EDUC	.07	20.46**	.05	5.29**	.01	.61	.05	6.41**	.02	1.20	.00	.15
SEX	-.15	-12.32**	-.13	-3.71**	-.10	-1.45	-.17	-6.57**	-.22	-2.80**	-.15	-1.73
ASIAN	.23	7.66**	-.03	-.19	.37	1.58	.14	1.37	.34	1.97*	.45	1.95*
HISPANIC	-.02	-.76	-.07	-1.13	-.13	-1.02	.08	1.87	-.02	-.16	.22	1.49
BLACK	-.12	-5.29**	-.06	-1.21	.17	1.40	-.05	-1.80	.01	.04	.09	.93
INGECL	.03	8.77**	.03	3.02**	.00	.18	.03	4.18**	.03	1.10	.05	2.17*
DISCUSS	.09	21.01**	.11	9.45**	.12	5.38**	.09	10.14**	.11	4.27**	.06	2.05*
FINCOME	.04	5.29**	.07	3.67**	.06	1.20	.05	4.49**	.01	.19	.06	1.81
SATISFY	.04	27.90**	.02	6.09**	.03	4.27**	.03	11.82**	.02	2.68**	.03	3.26**
Intercept	.36	4.72**	.22	1.09	.64	1.30	.54	4.21**	1.28	2.68**	1.09	2.43*
R²	.23		.16		.15		.16		.14		.12	

* = significant at .05 level; ** = significant at .01 level

TABLE 3.7 Parameter estimates for separate models relating background variables and other intervening variables to misbehavior within each family structure

Variables	M&F Coeff.	T	M&SF Coeff.	T	F&SM Coeff.	T	MO Coeff.	T	FO Coeff.	T	G/R Coeff.	T
PA_EDUC	-.04	-5.09**	-.02	-1.08	-.14	-3.10**	-.04	-2.41*	.01	.19	.10	1.50
SEX	.81	30.81**	1.09	13.83**	1.17	7.07**	.99	15.83**	1.18	5.89**	.91	3.82**
ASIAN	-.12	-1.76	.45	1.46	.08	.14	-.05	-.19	-.29	-.66	-1.43	-2.21*
HISPANIC	.13	2.87**	.26	1.86	.61	1.97*	.19	1.78	.31	.85	.15	.35
BLACK	.32	6.35**	.34	2.79**	.76	2.47**	.34	4.71**	.25	.73	-.10	-.37
INGECL	-.01	-.76	-.06	-2.46**	.05	.87	-.01	-.73	-.01	-.13	-.07	-1.07
DISCUSS	-.12	-13.06**	-.09	-3.17**	-.28	-4.87**	-.11	-5.16**	-.15	-2.36*	-.07	-.93
FINCOME	-.07	-4.54**	-.07	-1.41	.03	.28	-.06	-2.35*	.26	2.15*	.01	.10
SATISFY	-.04	-13.48**	-.05	-5.83**	-.03	-1.56	-.04	-6.54**	-.09	-4.05**	-.05	-2.36*
Intercept	7.31	44.57**	7.26	15.15**	8.66	7.07**	7.39	24.19**	4.46	3.68**	5.50	4.37**
R²	.13		.14		.20		.12		.15		.10	

* = significant at .05 level; ** = significant at .01 level

second, fifth, and eighth lines of Table 3.8, as the direct effect of family structure.

Standardized Test Scores. Although background characteristics and intervening variables are controlled and standardized to the overall means, the differences among different family types are still found, as in the previous comparisons in which the effect of intervening variables was not considered. What draws our interest, however, are the different degrees of change for some types of families, compared to the total effect of family structure measured by the first-step standardization method, as shown in line 1 of Table 3.8.

For example, for mother-stepfather and father only families, the estimated direct effects relative to test scores for mother-father families are about two-thirds to three-fifths of the total effects. These are no longer statistically significant (only 9% and 11% of one total standard deviation, respectively, for the two types of family structure). Interestingly enough (even to our surprise), MO shows an increment, rather than a decrement, to the estimated measure for mother-father families, although that difference is not statistically significant (only 2% of one total standard deviation). For other groups, father-stepmother and guardian headed families, the estimation still shows a substantial direct effect of family structure, not eliminated by controlling the intervening variables.

Next, what needs to be discussed is the reduction in the amount of difference compared to the estimation of total effect shown in Table 3.4.[16] Generally, the reduction in the amount of the difference can be attributed

TABLE 3.8 Direct, indirect, and total effect of family structure on student outcomes within each type of non-traditional family (estimated by differences of outcomes between traditional families and non-traditional families with backgrounds and intervening variables standardized)

Outcome Variables	Family structure				
	M&SF	F&SM	MO	FO	G/R
Test scores					
Total effect	-1.37	-1.95	-.97	-1.64	-4.29
Direct effect	-.91	-1.94	.16	-1.09	-3.10
Indirect effect	-.46	-.01	-1.13	-.55	-1.19
Grades					
Total effect	-.19	-.18	-.11	-.21	-.28
Direct effect	-.30	-.30	-.15	-.27	-.28
Indirect effect	+.11	+.12	+.04	+.06	.00
Misbehavior					
Total effect	.42	.58	.32	.34	.82
Direct effect	.30	.50	.35	.30	.86
Indirect effect	.12	.08	-.03	.04	-.04

to the intervening factors through which family structure has a portion of its effect. This is labeled "indirect effect" in Table 3.8. Among the types of non-traditional families, single mother families shows a large reduction, implying that the total decrement in test scores (relative to mother-father families) in single mother families is due to a lack of parental involvement and family income. This finding is consistent with the argument that the detrimental effects of a father's absence on children's cognitive performance are due to the negative function of some mediating factors used as intervening variables in this analysis (Shinn 1978). From this result, it might be appropriate to interpret that students in single mother families would not be disadvantaged compared to those in traditional families, at least in their achievement as measured by standardized test scores, if they are supported by the same level of family functioning, such as parental involvement, family income, and psychological well-being, as that in traditional families. To a lesser extent, if the family functioning were the same, the test score achievement of students in single father families and in mother-stepfather families would be closer to students' performance in traditional families. This can be seen in Table 3.8, where the size of the direct effect for these groups is somewhat smaller than the size of the total effect. Guardian headed families also show about 30% reduction but the difference is still the highest among non-traditional families, implying that the family structural effect still remains and is left unexplained by the intervening variables. The family type which shows the smallest indirect effect, leaving a substantial direct family structural effect is father-stepmother families.

Grades. The results regarding grades are of interest in that they contrast sharply with the results based upon the other two outcome variables. The point of importance is that there is no longer the pattern in which we can see the reduction in the amount of differences between traditional families and any of the non-traditional family types. The difference is expanding rather than reducing in relation to the comparison done in the examination of the total effects, even after all control variables are considered. This finding holds true across family types although there are some minor exceptions in guardian headed families.

How can we understand this? One conjecture is that intervening variables added for estimating the direct effect of family structure are not principal factors having to do with the negative impact on a student outcome measured particularly by grades. That is, all types of non-traditional families appear to give the strongest family structural impact on students' grades which is not explained satisfactorily by the variables controlled in the analysis. The comparison of the two standardized mean grades estimated for the calculation of both the total effect and the direct effect within each type of family structure supports this argument; there is hardly any significant difference between the two estimates.[17]

In sum, with regard to grades, all types of non-traditional families still show the negative differences, in descending order of single mother, single father, guardian, mother-stepfather, and father-stepmother families, from traditional families. Generalizing the findings, the two-parent non-traditional families are not better than the single parent families. Father-stepmother, mother-stepfather, single father, and single mother families appear to be less functional family types than mother-father families.

Misbehavior. Consistent with the comparisons regarding test scores and grades, the direct effect of non traditional family structure on misbehavior (relative to the effect of traditional family structure) is still shown in a negative direction even after the standardization of the intervening variables. The comparison of the total effect with the indirect effect also draws our attention. For mother-stepfather families, unlike the result in Table 3.4, it is shown that the overall effects of intervening variables explain a part of the family structural effect that was captured in the first process of comparison, i.e., the comparison of the raw difference. Elaborating on this point, about 6% of a total standard deviation is decreased in the estimated difference as compared to the raw difference: Dividing the amount of the decrement, $.39 - .30 = .09$, by the total standard deviation, 1.63, yields about .06. Table 3.8 also shows the largest indirect effect of mother-stepfather families among non-traditional family types. From this result, it is found that mother-stepfather families is different from traditional families in its family backgrounds and functioning (including parental involvement), and a comparison with Table 3.4 shows that a portion of the differences in misbehavior is due to differences in the intervening variables. Following mother-stepfather families, father-stepmother and father only families also show the direct effect of family structure to a lesser extent.

The direct effect of mother only families is about 21% of one total standard deviation, which shows a 1% increase compared to the total effect shown in Table 3.4. This 1% increase, which leads to a negative indirect effect of family structure as shown in Table 3.8, again gives us a puzzle as in the previous case for grades. Guardian headed families also show the largest direct family structural effect (53% of one total standard deviation) that is more than the total effect, resulting in a negative indirect effect of family structure. Inferences to be made regarding this result are: (1) These types of families may have other factors being associated with the negative effect on misbehavior that are not fully eliminated by controlling the intervening variables. (2) From the fact that some of the intervening variables are not significant when estimating their effect on misbehavior (see Table 3.7), we would argue that the background variables previously controlled for the estimation of the total effect, such as human capital in the family or demographic variables (gender, race or ethnicity), are more relevantly predicting student misbehavior for certain type of the family.

In sum, students in non-traditional families have higher levels of student misbehavior, which remains when differences due to their indirect effects through the intervening variables are controlled and standardized. Interestingly, more effects of family structure on student misbehavior due to the intervening variables, i.e., family functioning, are seen in melded families than in single parent families.

Explaining Functional Deficiency of Structurally Deficient Families by Means of Parental Involvement

From the preceding examination, we have found that non-traditional families are less successful in promoting better production of student outcomes. These effects are in part due to different degrees of parental involvement and the effects of other intervening variables such as family income and student psychological well-being. In part, they are independent of these intervening variables and can be regarded as direct effects of family structure.

We now turn to the final discussion, the task of which is to separate out the effect of the two forms of parental involvement on student outcomes from the overall effects of student backgrounds and of the intervening variables. In doing so, the general impact of family structure on intervening variables is estimated by regressing each intervening variable on the exogenous background variables and family type variables.

Family Structural Effect on Intervening Variables. In Table 3.9, we find that all coefficients of family composition variables are negative, and most are statistically significant. This means that each of these types of families are lower on each of these measures than are mother-father families: they are less likely to know parents of their children's friends (INGECL), they less often discuss school matters with their children, they have lower family income (except for father-stepmother families), and the psychological well-being of their children is lower. This supports the hypothesis that the structural effect of non-traditional families brings about a functional deficiency of those families in the production of student outcomes in the education of eighth graders.

The effect of parental education is significantly positive, implying that the increase in years of parental education contributes to the increase in the degree of the two forms of parental involvement, family income, and students' psychological well-being. For the two forms of parental involve-ment, all racial/ethnic minority groups are found to be related to lower measures than whites, suggesting that minority students do not get levels of parental involvement within the family context comparable to those of whites.

Among minorities, Asian American parents show the lowest degree of involvement with their children compared to other minority groups. As studies on Asian Americans' schooling reveal, parental involvement as defined here may not be the generally accepted forms of Asian American parents' educational involvement. They may resort to a different kind of parent-child relationship that may not be measured by the frequency of verbal communication with children or the degree of communication between parents and their children (Schneider et al. 1991). Minority group status, controlling on the other background factors, is related to lower family income. The effect of being minority on students' overall satisfac-tion, however, is quite opposite to that on the three other variables. African American students seem to have a higher degree of overall satisfaction about themselves than any other group. Asian Americans and Hispanics also have positive estimated coefficients, although not statistically signifi-cant.

Consistent with the previous findings are the relatively higher negative effects of guardian headed families on all intervening variables. Particu-

TABLE 3.9 Parameter estimates for models relating background variables and family structure to intervening variables

Ind. Var.	INGECL		DISCUSS		FINCOME		SATISFY	
	Coeff.	T	Coeff.	T	Coeff.	T	Coeff.	T
PA_EDUC	.13	22.96**	.16	29.55**	.18	52.28**	.23	13.15**
SEX	-.14	-6.07**	-.42	-19.64**	.03	2.17*	.64	9.22**
ASIAN	-1.09	-16.70**	-.38	-6.36**	-.28	-7.30**	.09	.44
HISPANIC	-.77	-18.84**	-.23	-6.11**	-.44	-18.60**	.13	1.06
BLACK	-.70	-18.81**	-.20	-5.96**	-.49	-22.81**	1.34	12.11**
M&SF	-.36	-9.36**	-.11	-3.14**	-.13	-5.98**	-.69	-6.01**
F&SM	-.91	-12.43**	-.25	-3.80**	.04	.87	-1.07	-4.92**
MO	-.23	-6.97**	-.11	-3.65**	-.86	-44.35**	-.53	-5.32**
FO	-.77	-9.35**	-.22	-2.98**	-.22	-4.61**	-..87	-3.56**
G/R	-.74	-9.31**	-.51	-7.01**	-.53	-11.57**	-1.10	-4.65**
Intercept	1.32	15.94**	5.36	71.16**	8.10	169.86**	13.68	55.69**
R^2	.11		.08		.31		.03	

* = significant at .05 level; ** = significant at .01 level

larly, they seem to be the most deficient family structure in terms of its functional relations with parental involvement in discussing school matters with students and of psychological well-being of students.[18] For parental involvement in "inter-generational closure" and family income, they have the second largest negative effect on them.

Comparing single-parent families and two-parent non-traditional families, the latter seem better only for family income. For variables other than family income, father-stepmother and single father families consistently show stronger negative effects than single mother and mother-stepfather families (between the two of them father-stepmother families are worse than single father families). This suggests that families in which the natural mother is absent are less functional in terms of parent involvement in the home and maintenance of students' psychological well-being than are families in which the natural father is absent. For these measures of family functioning, mother only families show the least functional deficiency of all the non-traditional family types. In other words, it seems that families with natural mothers are more likely to provide a more conducive home context for involvement than single father families and father-stepmother families. Moreover, there might be some estrangement between stepmothers and their children, leading both fathers and stepmothers to less parental involvement in the family.

Regarding family income, we find the reversed pattern among family types compared to the above discussion. As can be expected, controlling on the other variables in the table, single mother families have the lowest family income. The family with the second lowest family income is guardian headed families. The next lowest one is found in single father families. From this result it can be said that, putting aside guardian headed families, single parent families have lower family income than both-parent families when other background variables are controlled. It is also seen that there is no significant difference in family income level between mother-father families and father-stepmother families, in contrast to the comparisons for other intervening variables.

Parental Involvement and Its Effect on Student Outcomes. Non-traditional types of family structure are strongly related to the functional deficiency of the family and exert a negative influence on student outcomes directly and indirectly through the intervening variables. Another investigation of the relationship between family structure and each student outcome was carried out, focusing on the functional effect of only the two forms of parental involvement on student outcomes.

There are at least two virtues of doing this. First, by looking at the effect of parental involvement on students' education, holding other possible effects constant, we can understand the hypothesized relationship between structural deficiency and functional deficiency of the family in a more practical manner. In other words, understanding the effect of parental involvement would make it possible to identify the cause of functional deficiency of the family in terms of social capital available in the family. With this knowledge, we would be able to suggest some paths to improvement of educational outcomes regardless of a family's structural deficiency. Second, some policy implications are attached to this line of investigation, whereby the first virtue can be realized. Among the four characteristics of intervening variables examined in the previous section, the two forms of parental involvement, unlike family income or students' psychological well-being, can be regarded as the variables most accessible or responsive to educational policy.

The difference of the expected level of each outcome measure between the family with a high degree of parental involvement and that with a low degree of parental involvement was examined by using the regression equations presented in Tables 3.5 through 3.7 in order to investigate the effect of parental involvement on student outcomes. The estimated differences between student outcomes in the family with high parental involvement and those in the family with low parental involvement are presented in Table 3.10.

Regarding student achievement as measured by standardized test scores, it can be said that, except for mother-stepfather families, nontraditional families have a strongly negative impact on test scores which cannot be compensated for simply by more parental involvement in the family. Thus, this suggests the other possible source of functional deficiency in these types of families. Conversely, students in mother-stepfather families are likely to benefit from more parental involvement, even enough to make up for the discrepancy in the expected level of test scores as compared to the scores of students in mother-father families.

The effect of parental involvement on student grades within each family type has a pattern somewhat different from that for test scores. All types of families appear to benefit from high parental involvement for improvement of children's grades. The estimated differences are all about one standard deviation of grades.

Regarding student misbehavior, most types of families show differences of more than 50% of a total standard deviation, which are even more than that of mother-father families. This is a strong indication that an eighth grader's behavior in school is greatly affected by parental involvement.

Now, from these findings, we can derive some important arguments about the role of parents, in terms of their involvement in their child's

TABLE 3.10 Difference of student outcomes between the family with high parental involvement and the family with low parental involvement with control variables standardized for each family structure

Outcome variables	Family structure					
	M&F	M&SF	F&SM	MO	FO	G/R
Test scores	9.33	9.80	3.99	8.92	7.70	6.63
Grades	.69	.81	.72	.69	.81	.61
Misbehavior	-.77	-.84	-1.43	-.71	-.95	-.77

Note: See Appendix 3.3 for a technical explanation.

education or in terms of educational policy issues on parental involvement. First, all types of families, whether they are structurally disorganized or not, are found to be much better off in producing educational outcomes of their children if their involvement with their children's education is high rather than low. The positive signs for test scores and grades, and the negative signs for student misbehavior shown in Table 3.10 strongly support this argument. From this, it can be inferred that parental involvement functions positively for better student outcomes in non-traditional families, just as it does in traditional families. Second, when the results in Table 3.10 are compared to those in Table 3.8, it seems that a high degree of parental involvement in non-traditional families can compensate for the inferiority of student outcomes, in the sense that structural deficiency of families is strongly related to functional deficiency by lower parental involvement in children's education.

Conclusion

Unquestionably, the structure of the American family has undergone significant changes over the last thirty years. As a result of this, it is clear that many children experience multiple family compositions resulting from the transitory nature of the modern family. Recognizing these changes in the American family, the goal of this chapter is to determine how family structure affects student educational outcomes with the focus on the practice of parental involvement within each family structure. It is by this investigation that we can understand or unravel the mechanism by which family structure affects student outcomes.

Our results show that the average level of student outcomes varies according to different types of family structure. The average student in a traditional family scores well above the average student in any non-traditional family on standardized test scores, grades, and behavior. Thus, it appears that the non-traditional family structure exerts a significantly negative influence on student performance and behavior. This result is due not only to the different student background characteristics, but also to the lower levels of parent involvement as well as to lower family income and student psychological well-being. Parent involvement can be an efficient factor in non-traditional families for improving student outcomes. It is strongly suggested in this chapter that parental involvement can compensate to a certain extent for the negative effects of non-traditional families.

An encouraging corollary to this finding is the suggestion that the seemingly deficient functioning of non-traditional families, in term of children's education, can be compensated for by promoting more educational involvement of parents with their children's education: the development of more effective communication networks among parents of school children and an increase in parent-student contact for more frequent discussion about school activities or programs. Clearly, this possibility for the enhancement of student outcomes could contribute much to establishing educational policy that reintegrates the school, the families, and the communities in the face of an increasing number of educationally disadvantaged students.

Notes

1. The White House, Office of the Press Secretary, National Goals for Education, 1990.

2. Although other characteristics such as school-level variables also have very significant effects on student outcome measures, they are reserved for a more comprehensive analysis to be carried out later. Only variables which are thought to be directly related to family structure are now considered.

3. The family type of Mother & Guardian(s)/Relative(s) and Father & Guardian(s)/Relative(s) were grouped in the way described above but deleted in this analysis because very few students fell in these categories.

4. In tables, the mother & father family, the mother & stepfather family, the father & stepmother family, the mother only family, the father only family, and the guardian(s)/relative(s) family will be referred to as M&F, M&SF, F&SM, MO, FO, and G/R, respectively.

5. Native Americans are not included because of the small number of cases.

6. Many variables thought to be related to parenting practices occurring only within the context of the family were suggested and tried in the process of data analysis, but the three items presented in Table 3.A.1 were finally selected for their

consistency in interpretation and usability and reliability as characteristic variables for different family structure. For instance, items regarding a particular parent were considered but dropped since this analysis was done for different family structure that do not always have the same parent (mother, father) available. In addition, most of the dropped variables were insignificant either in the statistical sense or in the realistic application of them in the models.

7. Another statistical technique was also conducted for the comparison of the means within each type of family. For all three outcome measures, ONE WAY ANOVA testing the hypothesis that not all types of family structure are the same in their average outcome measures shows a very significant F-distribution probability (p-values for the three cases are .0000). This result supports the fact that student outcomes vary, on average, by family structure.

8. A higher value in misbehavior measurement implies a higher degree of students' misbehavior.

9. A similar argument was made by Astone and McLanahan (1991). Borrowing the concept of "social capital" postulated by Coleman (1988), they contended that "family income and the number of adults in the household are not the only factors that affect how well students navigate the schooling process" and that "the strength of the attachment between parent and child" should be taken into account, in addition to the number of parents in the household, as another indicator of children's "social capital" to interpret some negative findings about stepparent families. I agree with them generally but not with respect to their limited view of "social capital." According to them, social capital is merely "the relationship between the parent and child," quantified only by the number of parents in the household. This reveals only a part of the concept. Social capital should be understood by its function, that is, productive and facilitating certain actions for certain achievement of objectives (Coleman 1988, p. S98). That is, "social capital within the family depends not only on the physical presence of adults in the family but also on the attention given by the adults to the child" (Coleman 1988, p. S111).

10. When it comes to the apparent difference in educational outcomes between females and males, another question was raised: What would the gender differences within each family structural type look like in each racial/ethnic group? However, the results from the regression models relating family background characteristics, separately within each racial/ethnic group, including the interaction effect of students' gender and family structure, to each area of student outcomes did not show any clear picture of structure-specific gender effects. However, preliminary results suggest that there should be further analysis on the related issues, for example, about the effect of stepparents on child development or about the gender difference between girls and boys in their performance in certain types of family structure.

11. This paper is reminiscent of the type of research which aims to find the effects of family background, but is distinguished from others in that it focuses on the different parental involvement with one's child in education resulting from different family structure.

12. The technique used for standardization is explained in Appendix 3.2.

13. These results are generally the same as the findings from a single regression equation in which dummy variables are used for the type of family structure. But the measured effects from a single regression equation are smaller than those from the standardization method. This difference in the size of the effects is expected since the coefficients of a single regression equation are dominated by the effects of traditional families that have the largest number of cases.

14. Similar findings are presented in Garfinkel and McLanahan (1986).

15. The other two intervening variables, family income and psychological well-being, can also be termed as "financial capital" in the family and individual "psychological capital," respectively. In the earlier section, parent education was referred to as "human capital" in the family.

16. The change of a sign from minus to plus in the MO group can be regarded as a result from the great reduction in the sense of the absolute value. That is, the reduction of $|-.97| + |.16| = 1.13$, which is an almost 116% decrease in the difference.

17. The two standardized mean grades within each type of family structure are as follows:

	M&F	M&SF	F&SM	MO	FO	G/R
Background Variables Controlled	2.93	2.74	2.75	2.82	2.72	2.65
Background & Intervening Variables Controlled	3.03	2.73	2.73	2.88	2.76	2.75

18. R square of the regression equation for students' psychological well-being measure is only .03, which suggests that the principal effects are due to variables not included in the equation.

Appendix 3.1

TABLE 3.A.1 Description of variables and source items

Description of variables

Variable name	Description	Source
TEST SCORES	Standardized test scores composite (reading & matth)	BYTXCOMP
GRADES	Grades composite	BYGRADS
MISBEHAVIOR	Misbehavior composite scale	BYS55A,C,E,F
FAMTYPE	Type of family structure	BYP1A1,1A2
PA_EDUC	The highest level of parent's education (in yrs.)	BYS34A,34B
SEX	Gender of students (male, female)	SEX
RACE	Whites, African American, Hispanics, Asian American	RACE
INGECL	The number of parents of child's friends	BYP62B1,B2,B3,B4,B5
DISCUSS	Students' discussing school matters with parents	BYS36A,36B,36C
FINCONE	Family income	BYP80
SATISFY	Student psychological well-being composite	BYS44H,BYS56C,BYS56D

Description of source items

Source name	Description
BYTXCOMP	Standardized test composite (reading & math)
BYGRADS	Grades composite
BYS55A	Student was sent to office for misbehaving
BYS55C	Parents received warning about attendence
BYS55E	Parents received warning about behavior
BYS55F	Student got into fight with another student
BYP1A1	Respondent's relationship to 8th grader
BYP1A2	Partner's relationship to 8th grader
BYS34A	Father's highest level of education
BYS34B	Mother's highest level of education
BYP62B1	Parent knows parent(s) of child's 1st friend
BYP62B2	Parent knows parent(s) of child's 2nd friend
BYP62B3	Parent knows parent(s) of child's 3rd friend
BYP62B4	Parent knows parent(s) of child's 4th friend
BYP62B5	Parent knows parent(s) of child's 5th friend
BYS36A	Student discuss programs at school with parents
BYS36B	Student discuss school activities with parents
BYS36C	Student discuss things studied in class with parents
BYP80	Total family income from all sources 1987
BYS44H	On the whole, I am satisfied with myself
BYS56C	Students in class see me as a good student
BYS56D	Students in class see me as important

TABLE 3.A.2 Standard deviations of outcome variables within each type of family

Outcome variables	Total	Family structure					
		M&F	M&SF	F&SM	MO	FO	G/R
Test scores	9.96	9.94	9.46	8.99	9.73	10.14	8.78
(N)	(21,477)	(14,054)	(2,335)	(572)	(3,583)	(448)	(485)
Grades	.75	.73	.76	.73	.77	.77	.73
(N)	(21,943)	(14,365)	(2,364)	(582)	(3,681)	(456)	(496)
Misbehavior	1.63	1.50	1.75	1.87	1.81	1.96	2.01
(N)	(21,636)	(14,203)	(2,321)	(575)	(3,603)	(446)	(488)

The comparison of the standard deviation does not show any great fluctuation among family types, except for G/R, leading us to the interpretation that variations in students do not differ very much from one another in terms of family structure. By this finding, we may say that students are generally homogeneous across the types of families with respect to student outcomes. If this is the case, then we may go further to say that the student population is divided into different family categories without any predisposition pertaining to their cognitive achievement in school, implying that students (not in a particular level but all kinds of students in their achievement level) seem to have been generally exposed to the process of family disorganization. Family disorganization is taking place all over a variety of students in terms of their achievement level in education.

Appendix 3.2

After multivariate regression analysis is conducted using family background characteristics as control variables, the background characteristics of all students are standardized to the same average level, the means of the total sample. The objective of standardization is to equate the students in different family types, hypothetically, in terms of their family background. The technique used to calculate the expected outcome measures for the student with the average background characteristics in the total sample can be mathematically expressed as follows:

$$Y_j = a_j + \sum_{m=1}^{k} \overline{X}_m b_{mj}$$

where:

Y_j is the expected mean of an outcome variable in a family type j,

a_j is the intercept of the regression equation for a family type j,

b_{mj} is the coefficient of the mth background variable for a family type j,

$\overline{X}_m$ is the mean of the mth background variable for the whole sample.

The regression coefficients and the means of background variables are presented in Tables 3.A.3 through 3.A.6.

TABLE 3.A.3 Parameter estimates for separate models relating background variables to test scores within each family structure

	Total		Family structure											
			M&F		M&SF		F&SM		MO		FO		G/R	
Variables	Coeff.	T	Coeff.	T	Coeff.	T	Coeff.	T	Coeff.	T	Coeff.	T	Coeff.	T
PA_EDUC	1.57	48.12**	1.69	42.22**	1.38	13.10**	1.45	7.06**	1.12	13.42**	1.07	4.83**	.52	1.98*
SEX	-1.23	-9.33**	-1.33	-8.16**	-.56	-1.37	-.26	-.32	-1.23	-3.90**	-2.39	-2.41*	-.65	-.66
ASIAN	-.31	-.84	-.12	-.29	-1.66	-1.02	-3.01	-1.05	-2.93	-2.29*	.85	.38	-1.17	-.44
HISPANIC	-4.31	-18.73**	-4.13	-14.65**	-3.67	-5.04**	-5.90	-3.92**	-5.06	-9.40**	-5.15	-2.86**	-4.48	-2.61**
BLACK	-7.13	-35.25**	-6.90	-22.24**	-5.80	-9.18**	-5.77	-3.90**	-7.46	-21.25**	-8.51	-5.11**	-5.13	-4.85**
Intercept	31.33	69.37**	30.10	53.40**	32.37	22.76**	30.96	11.16**	36.98	33.86**	37.57	12.80**	41.01	12.37**
R^2	.20		.20		.13		.14		.19		.14		.09	

* = significant at .05 level; ** = significant at .01 level

TABLE 3.A.4 Parameter estimates for separate models relating background variables to grades within each family structure

	Total		M&F		M&SF		Family structure F&SM		MO		FO		G/R	
Variables	Coeff.	T	Coeff.	T	Coeff.	T	Coeff.	T	Coeff.	T	Coeff.	T	Coeff.	T
PA_EDUC	.10	38.42**	.10	33.37**	.08	9.51**	.05	2.78**	.08	10.93**	.05	3.06**	.03	1.25
SEX	-.17	-16.49**	-.16	-13.17**	-.16	-4.72**	-.10	-1.51	-.20	-7.66**	-.25	-3.18**	-.16	-1.91
ASIAN	.16	5.37**	.14	4.54**	-.10	-.76	.24	.97	.09	.81	.41	2.30*	.34	1.48
HISPANIC	-.07	-3.59**	-.08	-3.80**	-.13	-2.12*	-.19	-1.47	.03	.65	-.08	-.57	.20	1.34
BLACK	-.15	-9.55**	-.14	-5.97**	-.11	-2.14*	.18	1.41	-.07	-2.45**	-.02	-.12	.06	.71
Intercept	1.68	46.65**	1.69	39.01**	1.78	15.08**	2.12	8.91**	1.85	20.06**	2.17	9.34**	2.29	8.11**
R^2	.10		.11		.06		.03		.05		.06		.03	

* = significant at .05 level; ** = significant at .01 level

TABLE 3.A.5 Parameter estimates for separate models relating background variables to misbehavior within each family structure

| | | | | | | | Family structure | | | | | | | |
| | Total | | M&F | | M&SF | | F&SM | | MO | | FO | | G/R | |
Variables	Coeff.	T	Coeff.	T	Coeff.	T	Coeff.	T	Coeff.	T	Coeff.	T	Coeff.	T
PA_EDUC	-.09	-15.84**	-.08	-12.57**	-.06	-3.19**	-.19	-4.46**	-.08	-4.67**	-.01	-.13	.06	1.02
SEX	.91	39.76**	.83	32.09**	1.09	14.25**	1.20	7.25**	1.03	16.71**	1.11	5.62**	.91	3.99**
ASIAN	-.06	-1.01	-.04	-.55	.55	1.79	.33	.56	-.00	-.00	-.48	-1.09	-1.37	-2.21*
HISPANIC	.22	5.55**	.20	4.39**	.31	2.29*	.66	2.11*	.24	2.26*	.22	.62	.12	.31
BLACK	.42	12.12**	.34	6.79**	.35	2.93**	.72	2.35*	.34	4.97**	-.05	-.15	-.16	-.64
Intercept	5.75	73.51**	5.54	61.72**	5.53	20.75**	7.30	12.67**	5.75	26.94**	4.86	8.28**	4.56	5.92**
R^2	.10		.09		.11		.15		.09		.08		.07	

* = significant at .05 level; ** = significant at .01 level

TABLE 3.A.6 Means and standard deviations of control variables within each type of family

							Family structure							
	Total		M&F		M&SF		F&SM		MO		FO		G/R	
Variables	Mean	SD	Mean	SD	Mean	SD	Mean	SD	Mean	SD	Mean	SD	Mean	SD
TEST SCORES	50.462	9.96	51.645	9.94	49.288	9.46	49.148	8.99	47.745	9.73	49.024	10.14	44.777	8.78
GRADES	2.909	.75	3.003	.73	2.783	.76	2.720	.73	2.714	.77	2.743	.77	2.616	.73
MISBEHAVIOR	5.078	1.63	4.907	1.50	5.296	1.75	5.581	1.87	5.406	1.81	5.409	1.96	5.716	2.01
PA_EDUC	13.411	2.07	13.666	2.08	13.233	1.95	13.346	1.94	12.666	1.90	13.149	2.23	12.579	1.91
SEX	.500	.50	.503	.50	.475	.50	.579	.49	.482	.50	.573	.50	.515	.50
ASIAN AM	.034	.18	.041	.20	.016	.13	.020	.14	.015	.12	.051	.22	.037	.19
HISPANICS	.096	.29	.097	.30	.088	.28	.075	.26	.102	.30	.080	.27	.098	.30
AFRICAN AM	.126	.33	.075	.26	.121	.33	.078	.27	.306	.46	.096	.30	.374	.48
INGECL	2.715	1.66	2.910	1.63	2.500	1.59	1.985	1.63	2.405	1.66	2.040	1.70	1.819	1.72
DISCUSS	7.154	1.51	7.254	1.48	7.090	1.50	6.930	1.49	6.952	1.55	6.915	1.58	6.527	1.60
FINCOME	10.199	1.09	10.444	.91	10.221	.91	10.438	.73	9.302	1.35	10.127	.90	9.587	1.22
SATISFY	17.027	4.70	17.255	4.62	16.507	4.77	16.157	4.59	16.783	4.79	16.331	4.68	16.331	5.36

Appendix 3.3

Given the same degree of family background characteristics (PA_EDUC, SEX, RACE), of family income, and of psychological well-being, the expected student outcomes were estimated through the following steps both for the family with a high degree of parental involvement and for the family with a low degree of parental involvement.

$$\hat{y}_{j,PI(high)}=b_{j,0}+\Sigma b_{j,i}\overline{X}_{j,i}+b_{j,INGECL}X_{INGECL,(high)}+b_{j,DISCUSS}X_{DISCUSS,(high)}.$$

$$\hat{y}_{j,PI(low)}=b_{j,0}+\Sigma b_{j,i}\overline{X}_{j,i}+b_{j,INGECL}X_{INGECL,(low)}+b_{j,DISCUSS}X_{DISCUSS,(low)}.$$

Where $\hat{y}_{j,PI(high)}$ and $\hat{y}_{j,PI(low)}$ are the estimated student outcome measure within j type of the family with a high degree and a low degree of parental involvement, respectively. $b_{j,0}$ is the intercept of the regression equation in j; $b_{j,i}$ is the coefficient of ith control variable in j; $\overline{X}_{j,i}$ is the mean of ith control variable in j; $b_{j,INGECL}$ is the coefficient of INGECL in j; $b_{j,DISCUSS}$ is the coefficient of DISCUSS in j. Four values are given in the estimation. $X_{INGECL,(high)}$ and $X_{DISCUSS,(high)}$ are the 90th percentile of INGECL and DISCUSS, which are 5 and 9, respectively. $X_{INGECL,(low)}$ and $X_{DISCUSS,(low)}$ are the 10th percentile of INGECL and of DISCUSS, which are 0 and 3, respectively.

Using these equations, the difference of student outcomes within each family type, $D_{j,PI}$ is estimated by the following equation:

$$D_{j,PI}=\hat{y}_{j,PI(high)}-\hat{y}_{j,PI(low)}$$

$$=b_{j,INGECL}(X_{INGECL,(high)}-X_{INGECL,(low)})+b_{j,DISCUSS}(X_{DISCUSS,(high)}-X_{DISCUSS,(low)}).$$

Given that

$$X_{INGECL,(high)}=5,$$

$$X_{INGECL,(low)}=0,$$

$$X_{DISCUSS,(high)}=9, \text{ and}$$

$$X_{DISCUSS,(low)}=3.$$

Rewriting the equation,

$$D_{j,PI}=5(b_{j,INGECL})+6(b_{j,DISCUSS}).$$

4

Parent Involvement and Academic Achievement: An Analysis of Family Resources Available to the Child

Chandra Muller

We have seen in Chapter Two that there is a broad range of parental action which describes involvement in education. Chapter Three demonstrated analytically that involvement of parents can either enhance an already positive family structure or mitigate a potentially negative situation. Parent involvement has been treated as an intervening variable in the process by which family background affects academic performance. This chapter considers, analytically, a range of forms of involvement, how they are related to two measures of academic performance—achievement test scores and grades—and how they are constrained by available resources like income, education, and time. We consider involvement in three contexts: the home, community and school. The purpose of this chapter is to develop a broader understanding of the concept of parent involvement, both what constrains action and its impact on achievement test scores and grades. Thus, the central questions I address are two-fold. First, what are the similarities and differences in the associations between the forms of involvement and achievement test scores and the forms of involvement and grades? Second, are there discernible patterns in the associations of involvement with student background measures that might enhance our understanding of the important factors constraining involvement?

The positive relationship between parent involvement and student achievement has been documented by many empirical studies. Among them, Dornbusch, Ritter, Leiderman, Roberts, and Fraleigh (1987) found that parents with authoritative parenting styles have children who receive higher grades. Authoritative parenting is characterized by a combination of structure and discipline accompanied by open communication between parent and child. By concentrating more heavily on involvement which is directly related to the school, Stevenson and Baker (1987) found that parent involvement, as measured by teacher reports of parent attendance at PTO meetings and parent-teacher conferences, is positively associated with teacher evaluations of students. Fehrmann, Keith, and Reimers (1987), using the High School and Beyond data base, found that a parent involvement composite (which includes both involvement in home-based activities not directly related to school and involvement at school) is positively related to student grades. Lareau (1989) also found that teacher evaluations of students are enhanced if the students' parents were involved in school activities. Epstein (1991) found that those parents who engage at home in school-initiated, structured involvement activities designed to complement the school program have children whose reading achievement test scores improve at a faster rate over the course of the school year.

Several researchers have found that parent attributes typically associated with socioeconomic status (SES) are positively related to involvement. Lareau (1989) found that upper middle class parents are more likely to become engaged in school activities, especially in a proactive or controlling way, and that working class parents are more likely to take on a supportive and less involved role with respect to their involvement with their child's school. Stevenson and Baker (1987) found that teachers are more likely to report that parents participated in PTO and parent-teacher conferences when the mother's level of education is higher.[1] Baker and Stevenson (1986) found that mothers with higher levels of education are more likely to implement strategies for managing their children's transition to high school, are better informed about their children's performance, have more contact with their children's teachers, and are more likely to select college preparatory classes for their children (even when academic performance is controlled). Fehrmann, Keith, and Reimers (1987) found that SES is related to the parent involvement composite, but they also found that minority students have parents with higher levels of involvement when other background characteristics are controlled.

There have been changes in the family in the past several decades which could affect the way parents are involved in the child's education. One important change is that women with children have entered the labor force at high rates, and women tend to enter the labor force when their children are younger. In 1987, 70.6% of mothers with husbands present in the household and children between the ages of 6 and 17 years and 56.8% of those with husbands present and children under age 6 were in the labor force. This represents a 40% increase for mothers of older children and a 73% increase for mothers of younger children from the 1973 figures (the year many NELS students were born) when labor force participation rates of mothers with husbands present were only 50.1% and 32.7% for those with children ages 6 to 17 and younger than 6, respectively (U.S. Department of Labor, Bureau of Labor Statistics, 1989).

Labor force participation of the mother is likely to impact the resources available to the family and to the children. In fact, the decision to enter, re-enter, or never leave the labor force is likely to be one in which the mother weighs the needs of both herself and her family for financial, human, and social capital. How does one effectively balance the needs of the family? Employment will bring income but may cut into the time a mother may otherwise spend on family related activities. Is the mother's job taking her away from the home enough to deplete the social capital in the family, thereby removing the avenue by which financial and human capital (which may increase as a result of the mother's job) is conveyed from parent to child? The principal way I will examine resource constraints on parent involvement will be to analyze the impact of maternal labor force partici-pation on involvement. Labor force participation will be a measure of the time the mother has committed to non-family activities. In this way involvement is treated as intervening in the process by which family background affects academic achievement.

The underlying concern is the clarification of the mechanisms by which family background is related to performance. Thus, the way different kinds of parent involvement are related to performance is also of critical interest. The general plan of this chapter is to first examine the relationship of different forms of parent involvement to two measures of academic performance, student grades and scores on achievement tests. Differences in the ways parents are involved, depending on differences in the mother's labor force participation, will then be analyzed. (Descriptions of the variables used in these analyses can be found in Appendix 4.1.)

Academic Performance and Parent Involvement

A principal motivation for analyzing the forms of involvement in relation to two measures of academic performance, achievement test scores and grades, is to better understand the concept of parent involvement. While there is a strong relationship between the two measures, there are also important differences. For example, grades are assigned within the context of a classroom while achievement test scores are assigned accord-ing to a national standard. Grades are assigned by the student's teacher, who may base the grade in part on behavior or other subjective evaluation, whereas test scores simply reflect whether questions have been answered

FIGURE 4.1 Average grades of students by their achievement test scores and race/ethnicity

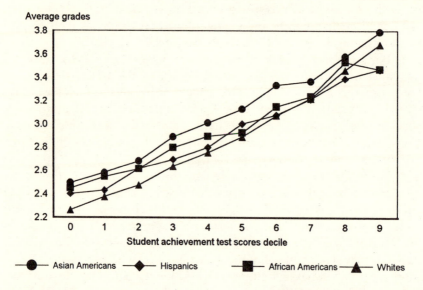

correctly. What follows is a brief analysis of the relationship between test scores and grades.

Figure 4.1 shows the relationship of test scores and grades by the race and ethnicity of the student. Here we see that for a given test score decile, the average grades of minority students are higher than those of whites, although there are some exceptions among those with the highest test scores. This discrepancy between grades and test scores has been identified as a source of "unrealistic aspirations" for African American students in the lower ranks. An example of this is encouraging them to expect to go to college. The discrepancy is most pronounced for Asian Americans, who tend to score higher on achievement tests and go to college. Their expectations are considered realistic even though they, too, have inflated grades relative to test scores.

One explanation for the discrepancy has to do with grades assigned to minorities by teachers. One might argue, for example, that minority students work harder, or that they are graded using less stringent standards. Figure 4.2 shows the relationship between the amount of time students report spending on homework per week and grades received. Here we see that for a given amount of homework time Hispanics and African Americans receive lower grades than Asian Americans and whites. In other words, on average an African American or Hispanic student would

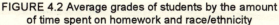

FIGURE 4.2 Average grades of students by the amount
of time spent on homework and race/ethnicity

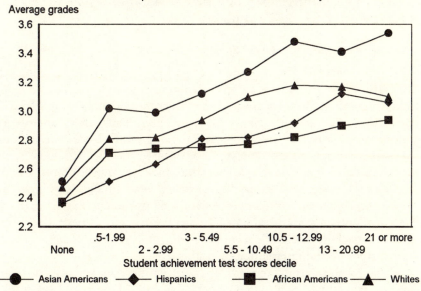

have to spend more time on homework for the same grade received by an Asian American or white student.

Clearly this is a complex process in which several factors are operating; to understand it fully would exceed the scope of this chapter. The relationship between achievement test scores and grades is no doubt mediated both by effort and context. Grades are a more subjective measure of academic performance than achievement test scores. In addition, grades may be more responsive to some kinds of action which indicate effort but do not directly impact the student's learning. That is, teachers may grade students partly on the basis of a subjective assessment related to the student's effort itself rather than on how that effort actually translates into learning.

Achievement test scores are less likely to be responsive to the subjective bias associated with grading by one teacher. They may, however, be affected by other bias inherent in the questions asked. For example, some argue that achievement tests suffer from cultural bias. Thus, neither grades nor test scores are perfect measures of intelligence or of what the child has learned in school; each has different weaknesses. The relationship of each to different forms of parent involvement should vary according to some of these differences. Moreover, since each of these measures is widely used to assess the child's performance and academic potential, the relationship of each to parent involvement is important. These are measures upon which decisions about the child's future are based.

Results for Achievement Test Scores

A principal objective in examining test scores, and grades as well, is to assess the relative impact of parents' attributes (like money, education, race and ethnicity, and time) on these performance measures, as compared with the actions that parents take with their child. Thus, there are several questions of interest. To what extent can the effects of conventional measures of background on test scores or on grades be explained by the actions parents take? Which parent actions make the most difference in the child's test scores and similarly in grades? And finally, how does the association between parent involvement and test scores compare to that of parent involvement and grades? To answer these questions I will first examine background and parent involvement in relation to achievement test scores and then in relation to grades.

Table 4.1 shows the standardized coefficients of four separate ordinary least squares (OLS) regressions on achievement test scores of background variables, with and without student grades, and with and without parent involvement variables included in the models.[2]

First, examining Column A, of the background variables included, the best predictor of the student's test score is the highest level of education completed by parents. Children from higher income families get higher test scores, but the influence of parents' education is about 60% greater than that of family income. Previous research has shown that whites and Asian Americans do better on achievement tests than Hispanics and African Americans, which is apparent in the table. Once grades are controlled (Columns B and D), the test scores of Asian Americans are also significantly lower than whites. On average, boys get lower test scores than girls.

We see in Table 4.1 a weak positive association between test scores and children from families in which the mother is employed part-time compared to full-time employment. There is no measurable difference between children of mothers not in the labor force and those employed full-time. Two of the variables included as controls because of their association with maternal employment have significant coefficients. Children of single mothers score higher on achievement tests, but this is due principally to the inclusion of family income as a control.[3] Also, children of older mothers tend to get higher test scores.

Of interest, then, is what happens when the parent involvement variables are added to the model, shown in Table 4.1, Column C. First, notice

TABLE 4.1 Regressions on achievement test score composite

Variable	Standardized coefficients			
	Column A	Column B	Column C	Column D
Parents' highest education	.283***	.064***	.150***	.049***
Family income	.165***	.051***	.135***	.096***
Asian American	.005	-.016**	.009	-.014**
Hispanic	-.086***	-.085***	-.075***	-.079***
African American	-.177***	-.173***	-.169***	-.166***
Urban	-.012	-.010	-.010	-.007
Suburban	.002	.023***	.010	.025***
Sex of student (male=1,female=0)	-.061***	-.012*	-.013*	-.009
Mother, stepfather	-.014*	-.006	-.001	-.001
Single mother	.051***	.060***	.052***	.060***
Part time	.033***	.021***	.017**	.015**
Not in labor force	.010	-.002	-.008	-.009
Mother's age	.025**	.021***	.013*	.016*
Number of siblings	-.003	-.0002	.001	.001
Student grades composite		.448***		.408***
Talk about current school experiences			.159***	.092***
Talk about high school program			.022***	-.012*
Frequency parents restrict television			.035***	.027***
Amount of after school supervision			.054***	.025***
Child enrolled in extra music class			.099***	.065***
Number of friends' parents known			.045***	.015**
Frequency parents contact school			-.124***	-.055***
PTO participation			.018**	-.011
Parent volunteers at school			-.005	-.010
Catholic school			.027***	.021***
Other religious school			.015*	.014**
Secular private school			.001	.002***
R²	.232	.409	.295	.425

* p < .05; ** p < .01; *** p < .001

that the amount of variance explained by the model increases from .232 to .295, suggesting that the actions parents take do more than simply explain the effect of conventional measures of family background on achievement test scores. They also explain a larger portion of the variance in the student scores.

When measures of parent involvement are included in the model, in Column C, coefficients associated with some background characteristics remain strongly associated with test scores, while others are significantly diminished. The negative associations for African Americans and Hispanics remain most stable with the addition of parent involvement measures into the model, indicating that differences in parental actions do little to explain the lower test scores of these subgroups. In other words, the actions of parents measured here have little to do with test score differences of African Americans and Hispanics compared to whites. The same may be said of test score differences between children in single mother families compared to those in intact families. The partial coefficient for single mother families remains strong and positive. A more thorough analysis of the effects of family composition on parent involvement and student performance is found in Chapter 3. These results are consistent with the findings of that chapter.

Perhaps the most striking reduction in a partial coefficient is that for boys. When parent involvement is included in the model (Column C), the difference between the test scores of boys and girls is greatly reduced so that boys' scores are almost as high as those of girls. The forms of parent involvement measured here explain nearly all the difference in test scores between boys and girls. It is difficult to say whether the gender differences in achievement might be a cause or effect of differential parent involvement. It is plausible to argue that parents treat boys and girls differently, and that those differences then affect the behavior of the child. It is equally possible to imagine that boys and girls act differently, that those actions are associated with their test scores, and that parents respond to the different behavior and needs of the child with different acts of involvement. Either explanation may account for the diminished significance of gender in explaining test score variation when parent involvement is added to the model.

When grades are added to a model which includes background only (Column B), there is a substantial reduction of the partial coefficient for gender even before parent involvement is added to the model. When involvement is added to the model which includes grades, there are no significant differences between boys and girls with respect to test performance. It may be that boys are graded lower, in part, because they have more behavior problems. To the extent that grades are a proxy for behavior problems (which are not directly measured in NELS:88), the introduction of grades is a control for behavior problems. Alternatively, it may be that teachers evaluate boys and girls differently, perhaps varying their evaluation of the student's effort depending on gender.

Parents who have different levels of education may become involved differently with their child's education, and in a general way the data seem to show this.[4] This could come about because parents with more education may place a higher value in education (having already invested more highly in it themselves) or it could come about as a direct result of the educational process of changing the parents' behavior. It may also be that parents with more education have differential access to resources not measured, which in turn facilitates their involvement. An example of this would be if schools or teachers respond differently to parents based upon the parents' level of education.[5] Epstein (1990) finds that teachers rate the involvement of parents higher as the level of parents' education increases. Nevertheless, even with the addition of involvement to the model, parents' highest education remains the best single predictor of test scores. Parents' actions also explain some of the relationship between family income and test scores. But, like parents' education, when involvement is included in the models (Columns B and D), family income remains a strong predictor of test scores.

The coefficient for mothers who work part-time remains significant, although reduced, when parent involvement is added to the model (Column C). The same may be said about the positive coefficient for mother's age. Children whose mothers are older and whose mothers work part-time tend to get slightly higher test scores compared with children whose mothers work full-time, even when parent involvement is held constant. These differences remain when student grades are included in the model as well (Column D).

Several forms of parent involvement are highly significant in predicting test scores. Talking about current experiences in school is strongly associated with higher test scores. Whether the child is enrolled in music class after school also makes a considerable difference in test scores. In both cases these are likely to be reflective of parents' attitudes regarding the educational process. When the educational process is more integrated into the everyday life of the family and the child, it may be manifest in higher levels of conversation about school activities and events and by spending time outside of school on extra educational activities, like music lessons (which not only include attending classes, but also practicing). These are forms of involvement that may come about because of general attitudes and values of the parents more than an intention to influence a particular aspect of the child's educational experience. Enrollment in music lessons is, no doubt, motivated by the parents' desire for the child to develop an understanding and appreciation for music. Learning music also symbolizes the learning of behaviors and values which are typically associated with success in school, like practice and drill, self-discipline, and performance.

Parents of children who perform better on achievement tests are much less likely to contact the school about academic matters. This finding is consistent with the notion that this form of involvement is motivated by specific academic problems (which students who have high ability will be less likely to have). Arguments about causality are problematic when it comes to achievement test scores. It seems unlikely that parent intervention would have such a strong negative effect. Rather, it seems probable that involvement comes about as a response to problems of the child. Yet the indication that parents' involvement is so responsive to the child's academic behavior throws into question any assumptions made about other forms of intervention which may have a positive relationship to outcomes. Are these forms of involvement also a function of the child's academic behavior, but in this case a positive response? It is impossible to answer this question. It seems plausible that activities that appear to be less directed at a particular consequence are also parental actions that are stimulated by a particular behavior of the student.

The other forms of involvement that are strongly associated with test scores are restriction of television on weekdays, adequate after school supervision, and parent friendship networks. When student grades are controlled, as shown in Column D, the association between parent friendship networks and student test scores remains significant and positive but is diminished in strength so that the partial standardized coefficient is comparable to that for mothers employed part-time and mother's age. Restricting television and after school supervision in some ways have to do with the environment of the family and all three may measure something about parental guidance and regulation of some of the behavior of the child. Television restriction is the most directed of the three forms of involvement, yet it is directed at structuring a climate and may in fact represent the imposition of broader parental values. The child's after school supervision is almost certainly related to the amount of structure a parent is in the position to impose on the child's environment. Coleman (1988) hypothesizes that one of the consequences of parent friendship networks is that common values and norms may be more easily enforced. The significant, positive Catholic school coefficient (and also that for other religious schools) may also be related to this "structured environment" dimension of parent involvement. However, secular private schools are not associated with higher achievement test scores, unless grades are controlled.

With the exception of contacting the school about academic matters, the forms of parent involvement that have the strongest relationships with test scores have more to do with what happens in the family than with parental ties to the school.[6] Parent participation in PTO is positively associated with test scores, although the association is not strong and becomes insignificant once grades are controlled. It is less important for predicting test scores than many of the other forms of involvement that have more to do with the family itself. While this is consistent with classical findings about achievement and the lack of importance of the school (e.g., Coleman et al. 1966), it nonetheless underscores the difference between what parents do and what schools do. In general, it seems that what parents do within the home makes a bigger impact on test scores than does what they do in relation to the school.

It may be that the things parents do within the home better reflect the things that they have been doing for a long time. Other activities, especially talking about current school experiences and music classes, may be measuring the same kinds of interactions measured by those studying parent interaction and development among preschoolers, only the substantive content of the interaction is adjusted for the age of the child.[7] It could be that these parent-child interactions best represent the historical aspects of the parent-child relationship and therefore represent a cumulative effect of involvement.

Results for Student Grades

As a measure of student performance, grades are more likely to have a subjective component than achievement test scores. They are assigned by teachers, and are usually relative to other students in the class or school. Grades are more likely to be related to actions which indicate effort but not necessarily effort that translates into learning that is measured by achievement tests. Thus, a comparison of the differences in the associations between parent involvement and grades, and parent involvement and test scores may clarify which actions of parents translate into performance which is based on knowledge of substantive material compared to the subjective evaluations made by teachers. There are three principal questions of interest with respect to grades. First, to what extent can the relationship between family background and grades be explained by parent involvement? Second, which parental actions are important predictors of student grades? And finally, how do the associations between parent involvement and grades compare with those of parent involvement and test scores?

Table 4.2 shows standardized coefficients from four regressions on student grades of background, and background and test scores, with and without parent involvement. Models in which the student's composite achievement test score is controlled are included because the primary interest here is in the impact of parent involvement on grades. The inclusion of test scores in some of the models allows for a comparison of the ways in which parental involvement influences grades independent of test scores. The amount of time per week spent on homework by the student is also included in each model. This is a control on the effort spent by the student on which the grade is in part based. If parent involvement translates into the student spending more time on homework, then that should be distinguished from involvement which does not have such a directly measurable consequence for student behavior.

Immediately noticeable in Table 4.2 is that the same family background variables (and the addition of homework time) explain about half the variance explained in test scores, .134 for grades (Column A, Table 4.2) versus .232 for test scores (Column A, Table 4.1).[8] The addition of measures of parent involvement to the models increases the amount of variance explained even more than it did for predicting test scores. In subtracting the R^2 for Column C from Column A in both Table 4.1 and Table 4.2, we see an increase of .088 when involvement is included in the grades models, compared with .062 for test scores.

The forms of parent involvement that are the best predictors of grades when achievement test scores are controlled (Column D) are the two forms of parent-child discussion. In contrast to its lack of importance for test scores, discussion about high school program planning is a highly significant factor in predicting student grades. Again the problem of direction of causality is evident. It would be reasonable to argue that good grades influence whether the parent thinks the child has the potential to do well later in school, and that as grades increase the parent is prompted to discuss future educational plans more frequently. Or one could argue that parents discuss high school program planning as a way to motivate the student to perform better in school, perhaps emphasizing the utility of higher performance for increasing opportunities.

Comparing either Columns B or D of Table 4.2 to the same columns of Table 4.1 suggests that parent ties to the school are more important for students' grades than test scores. PTO participation has a much stronger association with grades than test scores, as does talking about the child's high school program. In addition, whether the parent volunteers at school is a significant predictor of grades but not of test scores.

Choice of religious school (Catholic or other) has no association with the students' grades, in contrast to the positive association with test scores. Students who attend secular private schools tend to get lower grades,

TABLE 4.2 Regressions on student grade composite

Variable	Standardized coefficients			
	Column A	Column B	Column C	Column D
Parents' highest education	.199***	.064***	.150***	.049***
Family income	.132***	.051***	.096***	.036***
Asian American	.044***	.044***	.054***	.052***
Hispanic	-.001	.041	.012	.044***
African American	-.011	.079***	-.008	.068***
Urban	-.048***	-.042***	-.040***	-.037***
Suburban	-.046***	-.048***	-.037***	-.042***
Sex of student (male=1,female=0)	-.101***	-.075***	-.051***	-.047***
Homework hours per week	.127***	.057***	.078***	.033***
Mother, stepfather	-.043***	-.036***	-.026***	-.026***
Single mother	-.023***	-.048***	-.020**	-.043***
Part-time	.024***	.009	.004	-.003
Not in labor force	.026***	.022***	.003	.007
Mother's age	.002	-.007	-.009	-.014*
Number of siblings	-.007	-.005	-.000	-.001
Achievement test score composite		.504***		.449***
Talk about current school experiences			.153***	.088***
Talk about high school program			.078***	.071***
Frequency parents restrict television			.012	.001
Amount of after school supervision			.070***	.046***
Child enrolled in extra music class			.082***	.038***
Number of friends' parents known			..071***	.051***
Frequency parents contact school			-.168***	-.113***
PTO participation			.071***	.064***
Parent volunteers at school			.011	.015*
Catholic school			.012	.002
Other religious school			.002	-.004
Secular private school			-.022***	-.026***
R²	.134	.325	.222	.362

* p < .05; ** p < .01; *** p < .001

perhaps because the schools grade according to more stringent standards. Thus, as a form of involvement, choice of private school does not appear to be associated with a student receiving higher grades.

Provision of after school supervision, ties to parent acquaintance networks, and music classes have a significant, positive association with grades. As shown in Table 4.1, these forms of involvement make a difference in test scores, and independent of that, they also have a significant impact on grades. These measures may tap many dimensions of the concept of parent involvement. They are probably related to the amount of structure and learning-related activity in the child's environment. They may also measure the extent to which the family is integrated into a community which may or may not include the school. Context may be a factor here if, for example, there is differential availability of after school care and outside music classes. Similarly, communities may vary in the degree to which other parents are willing to engage in acquaintance relations.

Just as parents of students with low test scores contact the school at a high rate, parents of children who get bad grades are more likely to contact the school. The relationship is strongest when test scores are not controlled. When test scores are controlled, the relationship between parent contact of the school and grades still has the strongest association with grades of any measure of background or parent involvement included in the model. In other words, even when test scores are controlled, there is an extremely strong negative relationship between parental contact and grades. These are probably students who are either not working up to their ability (and are thus receiving low grades) or are being graded on a basis other than academic performance. In either case, it stands to reason that parents would reach out to the school.

There are some differences in the importance of some of the measures of background in predicting grades compared with predicting test scores.[9] First, notice that the higher grades of African Americans and Hispanics observed in Figure 4.1 is evident only when test scores are controlled. Column B of Table 4.2 indicates that for a given of test score, all minorities get higher grades, as was seen earlier in Figure 4.1. Thus, it may be said that for a given level of ability, the performance of minorities as indicated by grades exceeds that of whites. This is true even when the amount of effort as measured by their homework hours is controlled. In the case of African Americans and Hispanics it might be possible to attribute the difference to context. If grades are assigned relative to others in the school and if African Americans and Hispanics are segregated in schools or programs in which the average level of ability is lower than some national norm comparable to that used to assign test scores, then there may be a form of "grade inflation." Or teachers may have lower expectations of these students. Others argue that achievement tests tend to be culturally biased and do not reflect the ability of minorities as accurately. Thus, for minorities, grades would reflect achievement better than test scores.[10] The stability of the race and ethnicity coefficients, between models with and without parent involvement, suggests that differences in grades and in test scores of these subgroups are not due to differences in levels of parent involvement.

Parents' highest education and family income have a strong, positive effect on student grades, as they did for test scores. The effect is reduced substantially, although it is still strong, when student achievement test scores are included in the model. This indicates that a central way in which parents' education and family income lead to higher grades is by raising the child's academic ability, as reflected in higher test scores, although the increment cannot be completely attributed to that. When background, ability and involvement are all included in the model (displayed in Column D of Table 4.2), parents' education and family income are still significant predictors of student grades, although both forms of parent-child discussion, contacting the school, and PTO participation all have larger relative standardized coefficients. In part, the impact of parents' education and income on a child's academic performance can be explained by differences in the involvement of parents. It seems that parents act differently depending upon their education and income, but we do not know why. Certainly income is one reason. Some of these forms of involvement are contingent, in part, on the financial resources of parents. This is true of choice of private school and enrollment in extra music classes. Other forms of involvement, such as discussing current school experiences, are less so but are nevertheless associated with higher family incomes and levels of parent education.

While we saw that boys score lower on achievement tests than girls, the difference is even greater with respect to grades, a relationship that remains when test scores are controlled. Recall that the inclusion of parent involvement in the model predicting test scores greatly weakened the difference between test scores of boys and girls (the difference became marginally significant). This happens to a lesser extent with student grades. Apparently the difference between girls' and boys' grades cannot be attributed only to the things parents do. There is something more going on which could have to do with any number of things ranging from teacher bias on the basis of gender, to actual behavioral differences.

Finally, when only background variables and amount of homework time are in the model (Column A, Table 4.2) we see that children whose mothers are employed full-time attain lower grades. Both children of mothers who are employed part-time and those not in the labor force have higher grades. When test scores are controlled, in Column B, the difference between children of mothers employed part-time and full-time is no longer significant, suggesting that performance on achievement tests explains the grade difference. But children of mothers not in the labor force still receive higher grades. Other factors are operating for these children. When parent involvement is controlled, in Columns C and D, there are no significant differences between student grades based on their mothers' labor force participation. The actions taken by parents explain the labor force participation differences observed in Columns A and B. We know that test scores explain the difference in grades between those whose mothers are employed full-time and part-time, but not the difference between full-time and not in the labor force. It, therefore, seems likely that there may be a difference between mothers employed part-time and those not in the labor force with respect to the ways they are involved with their children, at least in how that involvement is associated with the children's grades. Some of these differences will be explored below.

Comparing Achievement Test Scores with Grade Results

The purpose of separately considering different forms of involvement in relation to test scores and grades is to develop insight into different ways parents become involved and the consequences of those different actions. Involvement appears to be of three sorts: (1) actions associated mainly with test scores, (2) actions associated mainly with grades, and (3) those actions which have strong associations with both test scores and independently with grades. In general, it is the home-and community-based involvement that is significantly related to test scores, and a combination of home-based and parent ties to the school that make a difference in grades. The forms of involvement that are good predictors of both grades and test scores may reflect more than one dimension of parent involvement. This section will review the findings about differences in involvement, and the performance measure with which they are most strongly associated.

The forms of involvement that are most important predictors of test scores tend to be home-based actions. Most important is discussion between parent and child about current school experiences. Although it is also an important predictor of grades, the role of this kind of discussion in predicting test scores is pronounced. The standardized partial coefficient for discussion of current school experiences is of about the same magnitude as that of family income. It is at least 60% larger than the second largest positive partial parent involvement coefficient, enrollment in outside music class.[11]

Enrollment in music class outside of school is strongly associated with test scores. It is also a good predictor of grades and will be discussed again when forms of involvement that are associated with both test scores and grades are considered. As a positive predictor of test scores, enrollment in music classes dwarfs all other forms of involvement except talking about current school experiences, discussed above. There may be a dimension related to enrollment in music class which is salient for performance on achievement tests. The other forms of involvement which are especially related to test scores are restriction of television watching on week days, and enrollment in Catholic and other religious schools. Taken together, these forms of involvement may indicate something about the home environment in which the child is raised. It may be an environment in which there is a certain amount of structure and discipline, and also a priority in education. These are all activities that indicate the child's time is structured, perhaps with an emphasis on educational activities. Music classes emphasize skills which increase success in all areas of academics—practice, self-discipline, logic, and performance.

The forms of involvement that are associated with both test scores and grades include enrollment in music class, provision of after school supervision, and parent friendship networks. These forms of involvement have to do with structure and discipline in the child's environment, at home more than at school. After school supervision is not provider specific, rather it simply measures the amount of adult supervision the child receives and in this way measures an aspect of the child's out-of-school activities. Parent friendship networks measure the extent to which the child's friendship networks include an intergenerational component of the parents. It may be that the intergenerational network provides a normative structure for the child's actions outside the home. Finally, both discussion of current school experiences and parent contact of the school about academic matters are two of the strongest predictors of both test scores and grades. However, discussion is more important for test scores and contact more important for grades.

Involvement which takes place outside the home, and especially involvement that includes ties to the child's school, characterizes the actions of parents that make the most difference in predicting grades. This includes PTO participation and volunteering. It is conceivable that students are graded, in part, on the basis of their parents' contribution to school activities. It seems that ties of parents to the school make more of a difference in the child's grades than test scores, although the causal direction of the relationship is difficult to determine. Does the parents' involvement at school raise the child's grades or does the parent become involved because the child is doing well? This question has not been answered.

The same question could be asked about talking about high school program planning, which also has a stronger relationship with grades than test scores. The amount parents and child discuss high school program planning is also a good predictor of grades. In contrast, it is a weak predictor of test scores and appears to differ in nature from the variable which measures discussion of current school experiences (which is a better predictor of academic success, especially test scores). It may be that discussion of high school program planning represents an attempt on the part of parents to manage an aspect of the child's school experience, while discussion of current school experiences represents a more general effort on the part of parents to share the child's experiences and incorporate them into family life. The forms of involvement that have to do with grades also tend to have a larger instrumental component, that is, the activity is more directed towards a particular objective. Discussion of high school program planning has this quality and Becker and Epstein (1982) find that parents who are involved in parent-teacher organizations have access through the meetings to information about how to help the child with schoolwork at home and information about what is taught in the classroom. Finally, enrollment of the child in secular private school is a negative predictor of grades. When grades are controlled it is a positive predictor of test scores. This is probably indicative of more stringent grading policies in these schools.

This chapter began by suggesting that parent involvement is an important intervening step by which the resources of parents are conveyed to the child in the form of involvement, which is then utilized by the child to improve academic performance. This implies that parents' involvement is at least in part constrained by the resources available to them. So far, there has been very little discussion of the constraints that are likely to be influencing involvement, beyond the inclusion of family resources as controls in the regression models. It is interesting to note that test scores are more often linked to the student's socioeconomic characteristics than are grades, and that these findings suggest that it is characteristics of the home environment that are most highly associated with test scores. It appears that it would be useful to understand the ways in which involvement is constrained by the resources of parents.

We saw that some resources are more related to parent involvement than others; their effect on performance is diminished when parent involvement is included in models predicting test scores or grades. In particular, this is true of parents' highest education, family income, student's gender and maternal employment. The decision of the mother to participate in the labor force is no doubt a result of weighing the needs of the family for financial, human, and social capital within the constraints imposed by the context of the family's circumstances. Presumably, the amount of time the mother spends at her job could have consequences for the ways she is involved with her child. At the very least, her family will have more money but less of her time available. The situation of every family is different; the reasons mothers enter or remain in the labor force may in some cases be determined almost solely by the family's need for the additional income, and in other cases by a desire of the mother for a career. In each case, however, it is probably an effort to balance individual and family needs within an opportunity structure. The relationship between the mother's employment status and involvement patterns will tell us something about constraints on parent involvement. Principally it will tell us about the constraint of time.

Time in Labor Force as a Constraint on Parent Involvement

We have seen that there are differences in the academic performance of children based on their mother's labor force participation. Children whose mothers are employed part-time tend to score higher on achievement tests, and both mothers employed part-time and those not in the labor force have children who receive higher grades. Most of these differences can be accounted for by differences in parent involvement, with the exception of the achievement test scores of students whose mothers are employed part-time. Even when parent involvement is in the model predicting achievement test scores there are differences between students whose mothers are employed full-time and part-time. There are unaccounted for differences in test scores between students based on whether their mothers are employed part-time.

It is possible that there are different factors operating which lead to differences in the children of part-time employed mothers and those not in the labor force. The results from the regressions on students' grades suggested there may be some differences between the way these mothers are involved with their children. Differences between the children of mothers employed full-time and those not in the labor force can be explained by differential parent involvement but cannot be attributed to differences in test score performance of the students. In contrast, test score performance can account for the differences in the grades of children whose mothers are employed part-time and full-time. Involvement of parents can also explain differences in grades between mothers employed part-time and full-time. These patterns suggest that there may be different ways in which mothers in each of the three employment categories get involved.

These three categories represent different amounts of time mothers spend at work outside the home. While it would be preferable to have more refined information about their labor force participation, for example, the number of hours spent at a job or the time of day (in particular if it is during the child's school day or otherwise), this information is not available from NELS:88. We also know nothing about the history of their labor force participation. Thus, this is a rough measure for the amount of time mothers have committed to activities outside the home. Nevertheless, these three categories of labor force participation provide some measure of the time demands on parents, and especially on mothers. Moreover, these time demands are probably fairly inflexible.

Eight Forms of Involvement Compared

Table 4.3 shows the standardized partial coefficients for employment status of the mother from regressions on each of eight forms of parent involvement.[12] The largest differences between activities based on employment status are in after school supervision and volunteering. These are the two forms of involvement which are probably most dependent upon non-flexible time. That is, parent engagement in these activities would be most likely to take place during the weekday, when most employed parents are at a job. The difference between families in which the mother is employed part-time compared to those not in the labor force is also most pronounced on these two activities. The standardized coefficient of after school supervision for mothers employed part-time is about one-third that of mothers not in the labor force, .058 compared to .154.[13] Time, along with child care opportunities, are probably principal factors in determining if and how long children are left unsupervised after school. There is also an ordered relationship in the amount of volunteering depending on time spent in the labor force, although the differences between mothers employed part-time and those not in the labor force are smaller than for after school supervision. This is indicated by coefficients of .084 and .105 for mothers employed part-time and those not in the labor force, respectively.

The levels of PTO participation of mothers employed part-time and those not in the labor force are equivalent, and higher than mothers employed full-time. The remaining forms of involvement, except contacting the school, have coefficients that suggest the largest differences in levels of involvement between mothers who work part-time and full-time.[14] Mothers employed part-time are most likely to enroll their children in extra music classes and they tend to know more of their children's friends' parents. The coefficients for discussion of current school experiences and restricting television are also largest for part-time employed mothers.

TABLE 4.3 Standardized regression coefficients for mothers employed part-time and those not in labor force (base is mothers employed full-time) from separate regressions of background characteristics on each of eight forms of parent involvement

Forms of involvement	Part time	Not in labor force	R^2
Talk about current school experiences	.028***	.016*	.069
Frequency parents restrict television	.047***	.039***	.048
Amount of after school supervision	.058***	.154***	.040
Child enrolled in extra music class	.029***	.004	.122
Number friends' parents known	.056***	.020**	.123
PTO participation	.031***	.031***	.102
Frequency parents contact school	.002	-.022**	.048
Parent volunteers at school	.084***	.105***	.055

* $p < .05$; ** $p < .01$; *** $p < .001$

Thus, it seems mothers employed part-time may have stronger community ties but also higher levels of involvement based in the family than mothers in either of the other two categories. The strength of community ties could be related to their part-time employment in several ways. Probably mothers employed part-time are likely to work near their place of residence, which makes it easier to get to know other parents.

The elevated levels of so many forms of involvement associated with part-time employment, especially compared to the levels of involvement for mothers not in the labor force, suggests that while time is a factor in constraining involvement it may not be the only factor driving these differences. These parents appear more likely to be involved in their child's education. The reason for the enhanced involvement is unclear.

Table 4.4 shows some demographic characteristics of mothers by labor force participation. Mothers employed part-time have higher family incomes, are slightly older and have more education than other mothers. They are also more likely to live in the suburbs. In contrast, mothers not in the labor force have the lowest family incomes, the lowest levels of education, and the most children at home. It is unlikely that the number of children at home accounts for the difference in involvement levels of part-time mothers and those not in the labor force since this variable is a control in the regressions presented in Table 4.3.

It may be that the higher levels of parental involvement when the mother is employed part-time indicate a greater propensity to allocate resources to the child's education; they have both an interest in doing so as well as the resources and opportunity.[15] If this is the case, then one could hardly make

TABLE 4.4 Characteristics of the mother and family by mother's employment status

Family characteristics	Full-time (n=10,685) (weighted 57.5%)	Part-time (n=3,747) (weighted 19.8%)	Homemaker (n=4,429) (weighted 22.7%)
Median family income	$32,285	$35,226	$30,396
Median age of mother (in years)	39.54	40.08	39.92
Median number of children at home	1.66	1.86	2.14
% high school graduates (mothers)	93.67	90.64	78.29
% college graduates	17.74	18.30	11.92
Urbanicity			
Urban	24.58	21.19	22.81
Suburban	42.85	48.66	44.72
Rural	32.57	30.15	32.47

the case that maternal employment affects parent involvement since the critical factor affecting both involvement and part-time employment is probably the presence of resources for allocation, the opportunity to engage in part-time employment, and an interest and priority of the parent in involvement in the child's education. In this formulation, part-time employment would be considered as an intervening variable, subject to many of the resource constraints such as income, education and opportunity, which are characteristic of the forms of involvement studied.

After School Supervision

As a form of involvement, after school supervision is different from the others we have considered. It has a remarkably low correlation with the other forms of involvement studied (correlations range from .091 with restricting television to .008 with Catholic school attendance), yet it has a sizable impact on the performance of the student. The amount of time spent unsupervised after school has a clear, negative relationship with test scores and, independently, with grades. And it is related to the amount of time mothers spend in the labor force. The R^2 for the model predicting amount of after school supervision is low, only .04, indicating that most of the variation is not explained by the background variables measured. It may be that the availability of child care options is vastly different for different families and for different areas. There is no measure in NELS:88 of after school care options; thus it must be left to speculation whether opportunity would help explain variation in time spent after school.

An important question to ask concerns the extent to which differences in performance measures can be explained simply by differences in background and after school care. In other words, we must assume that constraints on this form of involvement vary a great deal, depending upon availability of alternatives. But the question remains, in light of those constraints, how much of the estimated difference in academic performance of children based on maternal employment status can be explained only by differences in after school supervision? It is to this question that we turn next.

We saw in Tables 4.1 and 4.2 that the inclusion of parent involvement in models predicting grades diminished to insignificance any predictive power of employment status and diminished the difference between part-time and full-time mothers when predicting grades. Let us now consider only the role of after school supervision in the relationship between employment status and performance. Can the inclusion of after school supervision alone in a model in which background variables predict performance reduce the difference between mothers employed full-time and part-time and those not in the labor force? Table 4.5 shows only the coefficients in question. After school supervision alone accounts for the difference in student grades between those not in the labor force and mothers employed full-time when test scores are not controlled. When test scores are included in the model a difference again exists, but the magnitude of the association is less and the significance level is lowered. Thus, it seems that a major portion of the difference between mothers not in the labor force and those employed full-time with respect to the grades of their child may be attributed simply to difference in after school supervision.[16]

Differences between mothers employed part-time and the others are a different matter. Children of mothers employed part-time still have significantly higher grades and test scores, even when after school supervision is included in the model. It appears that other factors are driving the differences between academic performance of children whose mothers are employed full-time and part-time. Previous results presented above suggest that mothers employed part-time engage in other forms of involvement at higher rates than mothers employed full-time, and apparently these have more to do with the difference. Those actions account for grade differences but not differences in test scores. It is impossible with the information available to explain those differences. For example, it may be that the labor force participation of mothers employed part-time and full-time is different, and that labor force participation before the child entered school plays a role in explaining test score differences.[17]

TABLE 4.5 Selected standardized coefficients for regressions on student test scores and grades, with and without after school supervision included in models containing background controls

Mother characteristics	Test scores		Test scores (grades controlled)		Grades		Grades (test scores controlled)	
Part time employment	.033***	.029***	.021***	.020**	.026***	.021**	.009	.006
Mother not in labor force	.010	-.001	-.002	-.007	.028***	.014	.023***	.015*
After school supervision		.073***		.032***		.093***		.056***
R^2	.232	.237	.409	.410	.119	.127	.322	.325

* $p < .05$; ** $p < .01$; *** $p < .001$

Conclusion

In comparing parent actions in relation to test scores and grades it is apparent that the concept of parent involvement has multiple dimensions. Some actions take place inside the home or within the community and others are associated with school ties. For instance, talking with the child about current school activities, restricting television, after school supervision, parent friendship networks, and music classes are all based either in the home or community. And each is strongly associated with the child's test scores.

In contrast, the forms of involvement that are more strongly associated with a student's grades are those which include parent relations with the school, like PTO participation and volunteering at the school. Some kinds of involvement in the home and community are also important predictors of student grades. Parent-child discussion about both current school experiences and high school program planning, parent friendship networks, music classes, and after school supervision all fall into this category. That parent discussion about high school program planning, PTO participation, and volunteering have more to do with grades than test scores suggests that these activities may have an instrumental component, designed to influence a particular circumstance of the student. In most cases it probably reflects an attempt by parents to influence how the child's performance is evaluated at school or the consequences of the evaluation.

The distinction between home-, community-, and school-based involvement provides insight into the ways parents' resources and contextual circumstances may influence involvement. Each context is likely to constrain or facilitate involvement in different ways. Home-based involvement may reflect resource constraints from things like family income, but it seems to be constrained less by parents' time, at least as measured by the employment status of the mother. Involvement outside the home will be constrained by the parents' opportunity structure. For instance, whether a parent develops acquaintance ties with other parents will depend in part upon the willingness of other parents to engage in those relations. Likewise, parent involvement in the school may depend upon the extent to which the school encourages or discourages such action. Thus, in considering who engages in what actions there are two important factors to consider: the impact of resource and opportunity constraints on action and the interest or priority of parents for engaging in such actions.

The examination of the relationship of maternal employment status with parent involvement provides insight into one way in which interest in involvement and resource constraints might be balanced differently by parents. Parents in families in which the mother works part-time tend to engage at a higher rate in all forms of involvement which have a proactive, positive relationship with the child's performance. Except for after school supervision and volunteering at school (both of which appear related to the time available to mothers), these parents have the highest levels of involvement irrespective of maternal employment status. Thus, one must question whether these mothers are not adjusting for their employment status to either the needs of the child or their interest in involvement with their child's education. If mothers do work part-time as a way to juggle needs for time, money, and possibly career, then one can hardly make the case that employment status *causes* involvement. Rather, like involvement, it may be subject to resource constraints of parents.

Policy implications from these findings fall into two categories: those related to the constraints implied by mother's labor force participation and those related to the general findings about parent involvement. Some women no doubt have interests which resemble those of the mothers who work part-time but do not have the resources or opportunity to work reduced hours. It may be that flexible work hours for parents would be something that helps the child and should be made more widely available to parents. This would give parents more options and would probably be most important for single mothers and children in low and moderate income families, since it is these families that are most likely to be in the position where mothers must work full-time because of financial and opportunity constraints.

Volunteering in school and the amount of time a child is left unsupervised are related to time constraints from labor force participation. But volunteering has only a weak relationship with grades. After school supervision, on the other hand, is strongly related to a child's test scores, and when those are held constant, it has a significant and powerful independent effect on grades.[18] It seems that families need after school care options, possibly even for children as old as eighth grade. Moderate levels of after school supervision probably provide the child with a structure and regulation of activity which enhances performance.[19] As more families have both parents in the labor force and there are more single parent families, this need has probably become more pronounced. Provision of after school supervision would probably most benefit children in single parent households and in low income families, since the decision of those parents to work is more heavily contingent upon the financial needs of the family.

The policy implications from the findings that there are extensive differences in the ways parents become involved are less specific and imply a note of caution more than a particular recommendation. The process by which parent involvement leads to higher achievement levels of students is almost certainly a complex one in which parents' resources, interests, and structure of opportunities are all important factors. That parent involvement is multifaceted means that policy which simply encourages parent involvement may not have the assumed positive consequences. Involvement which takes place within the school, particularly that which appears to have a well-defined, instrumental objective, may raise the child's grades but does very little to raise the child's test scores. There are forms of involvement which appear to be associated more directly with test scores, and probably with learning. It may serve the interests of children if policy makers concentrate on encouraging these forms of involvement as well.

Notes

1. It may be important to distinguish between parent reported activity and teacher reported activity. For instance, Epstein (1990) found that single mothers reported more requests by teachers for involvement, and they reported higher levels of involvement activity, however teachers rated parents' involvement activity as more frequent if parents were married, and more effective if the parents had higher levels of education.

2. In each model pairwise deletion was used. All regressions are weighted and the sample standard errors are adjusted by the average design effect of 1.56. This applies to all regressions presented in this chapter. A correlation matrix used to estimate the regressions presented in the text may be found in Table 4.A.4 of Appendix 4.1.

3. Families in which a single mother is the head of household have especially low incomes, so that the positive coefficient is probably because these children are compared with other children who have lower levels of other SES related characteristics which are not controlled in the model. If family income is excluded from

the model, the coefficient for single mothers is significantly lower, and the coefficient for parents' highest education is much larger. If an SES composite is used as a control, there is no appreciable difference between children of single mothers and those in two-natural-parent families.

4. This does not mean that parents' education makes a difference in every form of involvement. To examine this we would need to analyze each form separately. This has been done somewhat in Chapter 2 of this book and more extensively in Muller (1991). Results indicate that parents' highest education is extremely important in predicting involvement, and that there are differences in the association between parents' education and involvement. In general, parents' education is more important in predicting the forms of involvement which are most closely associated with test scores, basically the forms of involvement that have to do with aspects of the home environment. The exception is in after school supervision, which is not strongly associated with parents' education. Parents' highest education is less associated with involvement with the school.

5. Some have suggested that parents' education helps the child because parents with higher levels of education become involved in more effective ways (efficacy is indicated by higher associated achievement of their child). There is very little evidence of that in these data. An example of such an argument is in Baker and Stevenson (1987) who find that more highly educated mothers engage in more interactions with the school to manage their child's transition to high school. Efforts to model an analogous process for predicting either test scores or grades by adding an interaction term which includes either the parents' highest education or the mother's highest education and parent involvement have not produced any consistently significant results.

6. It is interesting that the one home-based activity which is probably directed at guiding the child in school related issues directed talking with a parent about high school program, while significant, is not a particularly strong predictor of achievement test scores. It is discussion which is highly focused on a particular outcome. What is more, when grades are controlled (and also the level of talking about current school experiences is controlled) the coefficient for directed talking becomes negative and significant (Column D). At this point it is difficult to disentangle talking about current school experiences from discussion designed to influence the child's high school program, although there are differences between the two activities, suggested by a correlation between the two of only .329.

7. For example, the Home Observation for Measurement of the Environment (Caldwell and Bradley 1984) measures mother child interactions, such as the frequency the mother talks to the child, and whether the mother answers her child's questions or requests verbally.

8. When amount of homework is not in the grades model (which makes the independent variables identical to the model in Column A of Table 4.1), the R^2 is .119.

9. The controls for urbanicity are mostly in the model to control regional differences in availability of resources that might influence involvement; however it should be noted that students in non-rural areas get significantly lower grades.

10. It is interesting to note that separate regressions for public school and Catholic school indicate that differences of African Americans and Hispanics from whites are markedly less in Catholic school. These regressions may be found in Table 4.A.3 of Appendix 4.1. In the Catholic school regression the coefficient for homework is also smaller. (The average amount of homework done by Catholic schools is higher and the standard deviation smaller, as well.) It seems that in Catholic schools, students may be more likely to work up to their ability regardless of race. What is more, they may be more likely to be graded more on their performance than other factors.

11. Contacting the school about academics has a larger negative partial coefficient when grades are not controlled, but it is involvement of a different sort, probably intervention in a problem.

12. For ease of presentation I have used OLS to estimate the parameters of the dichotomous enrollment in music classes and parent volunteers at school variables. The background variables included in these models are the same as those included in the regressions in Table 4.1. Twenty percent of the parents volunteer and 26% of students are enrolled in music classes, thus the estimates should be fairly stable, and in fact logistic regressions indicate similar results. Several measures of parent involvement examined in the previous sections have been excluded here. Discussion about high school program planning was excluded because the R^2 for the regression was only .026. The pattern exhibited in the coefficients of employment status follow much the same pattern as those of discussion of current school experiences. Also, parent choice of school sector variables were not included because the results contributed very little additional information to the question at hand and the percentage of children attending those schools is low, only 7.7% attend Catholic school, 3% attend other religious school, and 1.6% attend secular private school. Mother's employment status is not a principal factor in parents' school choice.

13. The after school supervision variable is coded so that a larger coefficient indicates more supervised time after school.

14. It is only in contacting the school that there is no difference with families in which the mother is employed full-time and part-time. And mothers not in the labor force engage in the activity significantly less often than the others. Contacting the school about academic matters is probably an intervention activity in which parents are most likely to engage when their child is having a problem. The other forms of involvement all have a stronger component which is proactive, and there is a positive relationship between involvement and achievement. Thus, contact is likely to take place when the need arises. Rather than an action taken as a matter

of course, it is an action which is highly targeted and as such probably depends heavily on the particular circumstances of the child.

15. When the involvement levels of subsets of mothers are examined, not presented here, similar patterns according to employment status are evident. For example, single mothers with moderate levels of education have similar patterns of involvement if one characterizes them by employment status. There are some interesting differences in levels of involvement depending on the gender of the child. For example, especially among parents with moderate and lower levels of income or education, girls are more likely to be left unsupervised after school than boys. Exploring these differences is beyond the scope of this chapter.

16. These results are consistent with Muller, Schiller, and Lee (1991) who showed that academic performance of children whose mothers work full-time could be significantly improved if they were not left unsupervised for long periods.

17. Coleman, Hoffer, and Kilgore (1982) found that only maternal employment before the child entered school influenced achievement test scores.

18. The association measured here may reflect a cumulative effect. Probably the children who are left for long hours unsupervised now include those children who were also left at an earlier age. Thus, the strength of the effect could easily be increased because of a cumulative detrimental impact. The data do not allow for an examination of this conjecture.

19. Muller, Schiller, and Lee (1991) found that moderate levels of time left unsupervised were not negatively associated with academic performance. Rather it is in extended hours that problems arise.

Appendix 4.1

Explanation of the Measures

Parent Involvement

Effort has been made to select a diverse set of measures of parent involvement for analysis. These include five home-based measures and five that measure ties between parents and the child's community and/or school. The home-based measures are (1) the frequency parents and child discuss the child's current school experiences; (2) the frequency they discuss high school program planning; (3) the amount parents restrict the child's television watching on weekdays; (4) the average number of hours the child is left unsupervised after school; and (5) whether the child is enrolled in extra music classes. Parent relations outside the home include parent ties to the social community of the child which are measured by (6) the number of parents of the child's friends who are known by the parent; and four ways parents interact with the school including (7) the frequency parents contact the school about academic matters; (8) the level of parent participation in a parent-teacher organization (PTO); (9) whether the parent volunteers at the school; and (10) whether the parents exercise choice by sending their child to private school (three types of private school are identified as Catholic, other religious or secular private school).

Academic Performance

Two measures of academic performance are used as dependent variables. The first is a composite of the reading and mathematics achievement test scores compiled by NCES. The composite is based upon the student's performance on the reading and mathematics achievement tests administered as part of the student interview. For the second, grades, students in NELS:88 were asked to report their grades "from sixth grade up till now" in four subject areas (English, mathematics, science, and social studies).[1] From these self-reports, NCES constructed a composite average in which all subjects are weighted equally to produce a variable ranging from .5 to 4.0 (A student report that grades for a subject are "mostly below D's" was assigned a value of .5.)

Family Background

Mothers are classified according to whether they work full-time, part-time, or not in the labor force and claim to be homemakers when asked about employment and occupation. Maternal employment and all other variables are described in Table 4.A1. There are other activities in which mothers may engage that do not fall into any of these categories. For example, a mother may be a student, retired, or unemployed and looking for a job. None of these has enough women to warrant an additional employment category for the analysis, yet they are different enough from the other groups that they should not be included in any existing categories. Therefore, women who were not identified in the questionnaire as falling into one of the three categories were excluded from analysis.[2]

Other background variables used throughout the analyses fall into two categories. There are those which are known to be important predictors of academic performance. Others are important for this analysis because they are associated with maternal employment status. Parents' highest education,[3] family income, race and ethnicity, urbanicity, and the student's gender fall into the first category. In the second category the variables are adult family composition,[4] the mother's age, and the number of siblings who live in the (student) respondent's home. Mothers who are employed tend to be younger, have fewer children, and be in non-intact families. They also tend to be more highly educated. While not a background measure, the number of homework hours done by the student per week is also included in some of the models. It is a composite measure constructed by NCES of student reports of the number of homework hours in each subject. The composite is the total hours spent on homework per week for all subjects.

Notes for Appendix 4.1

1. Since this measure has a historical and cumulative component because students were asked about their grades over almost a three year period, it is conceivable that the student's grades affect his or her score on the achievement test administered for NELS:88. This could come about if a student is tracked according to grades given in the sixth or seventh grade, from which the student would then have been provided with more or less opportunity for learning material relevant to test performance.

2. This definition of employment status contributes somewhat to the disproportionate representation of families of higher SES in the analysis. The main findings in the analyses which follow are present whether or not these students are excluded from analysis. This provides a sample which is slightly different from the total sample. The weighted percentages of cases according to availability of information on mothers' employment status by SES quartiles and race and ethnicity may be found in Table 4.A.2. Lower SES families and racial and ethnic minorities are excluded at a higher rate from this analysis. This exclusion reduces the total sample size considered to 18,861 observations.

3. I have chosen to control for the parents' highest level of education instead of the mother's educational attainment for several reasons. First, the data do not allow for controls of both because the correlation between the two is too high. Exploratory analysis indicates that parents' level of involvement is more strongly

associated with parents' highest education than with mother's highest education. Since the principal focus is on parental involvement rather than why mothers work, it is most important to control on the factor most highly associated with parental involvement.

4. Here, I will only consider three family types: intact families in which the child lives with both parents, families in which the child lives with his or her natural mother and stepfather, and single mother families. This will allow for a direct linkage between labor force participation and the mother in question. It would be impossible in considering stepmother-father families with these data to assess whether the mother referred to in the employment status variable is the stepmother or natural mother or to assess the relative role of each in the child's life, thus stepmother-father families must be excluded from analysis of family composition. Stepmother-father families comprise only 2.2% of the sample of mothers with known employment status.

Appendix 4.2

Description of Variables

Student Background

Parents' highest education. Constructed by NCES. Level of education of parent with most education. Six-point scale from 1=did not finish high school to 6=Ph.D., M.D., other.

Family income. Parent report. Ranges from 1=None to 15=$200,000 or more.

Race and ethnicity. Dummies for Asian, Hispanic, and African American not of Hispanic origin created from an NCES construct. Base is white, not Hispanic.

Urbanicity. Urbanicity of the school. Dummies for urban and suburban, base is rural.

Sex of student. Student report, female=0, male=1.

Family composition. Constructed by NCES. Dummies stepfather, natural mother families and single mother families. Two-natural parent families are the base and other family types are excluded from analysis.

Mother's age. Constructed from parent report of the range of years in which the mother's birth year falls; midpoint of interval is used to calculate her age in 1988. Range is 28 to 59.5.

Number of siblings. Parent report of number of children in the home unless it is unavailable, in which case student report of number of siblings is substituted. Range is 0 to 6.

Maternal employment status. Parent response about the employment status of the mother. Responses of working full-time, part-time and homemaker were used. Parents with other responses are excluded from analysis. Dummies are created, with full-time category as base.

Homework hours. NCES composite of student report of number of hours spent on homework per week.

Parent Involvement

Talk about current school experiences. Constructed from student responses to the questions "Since the beginning of the school year, how often have you discussed the following with either or both of your parents/or guardians?" (1) "school activities", and (2) "things you've studied in class". Responses were summed to range from 0 to 4 and divided by two, thus the variable construct ranges from 0 to 2. The category for a single variable with the value of 0 represents a response category of "not at all" and a 2 represents "three or more times."

Talk about high school program. Constructed from student responses about the frequency with which the student has talked with the (1) father or (2) mother "about planning your high school program." If the student response to the question of talking with the father was greater than zero, then the value for that response was used. Otherwise the response for talking with the mother was used. The range is 0 to 2, with 0="not at all" and 2="three or more times."

Frequency parents restrict TV. Student response to the question "How often do your parents or guardian limit the amount of time you can spend watching TV." Responses were coded so that a zero represents "never" and 3 represents "often."

After school supervision. Constructed from the student response to the question "On average, how much time do you spend after school each day at home with no adult present?" The variable is coded -4="more than three hours" and 0="none—never happens."

Extra music class. Parent response to the question "Has your eighth grader attended classes outside of his or her regular school to study any of the following?—music" 1=attended, 0=not attended.

Friends' parents known. Summation of the the parents of the child's friends known. Parents were first asked to identify the first names of up to five of the child's friends. Then parents were asked "whether you know the parents of that child." The variable was coded "yes"=1, "no"=0. Responses of "yes" were summed so range is 0 to 5.

Frequency parents contact school. Constructed from parent responses to two questions "Since your eighth grader's school opened last fall, how many times have you or your spouse/partner contacted the school about each of the following:" (1) "Your eighth grader's academic performance?"; and (2) "Your eighth grader's academic program for this year?". Two response categories, "Three or four times" and "More than four times," are combined and the variables rescaled to range from 0 to 2 where 0=none. The two responses are then summed to produce a variable ranging from 0 to 4.

PTO participation. Constructed from parent responses to the questions: "Do you and your spouse/partner do any of the following at your eighth grader's school?" (1) "Belong to a parent-teacher organization"; (2) "Attend meetings of a parent-teacher organization"; and (3) "Take part in the activities of a parent-teacher organization". Responses are 1=yes, 0=no and summed for a variable ranging from 0 to 3;

Parent volunteers at school. Parent response to "Do you and your spouse/partner do any of the following at your eighth grader's school?—Act as a volunteer at the school." Responses are 1=yes, 0=no.

School sector choice. Three dummies (base is public school) are constructed from the NCES designation of school sector.

Table 4.A.1 Availability of mother's employment status by SES and race/ethnicity

Mother's status	SES Quartile				Race/Ethnicity			
	Low	2	3	High	Asian	Hispanic	African American	Whites
Employment status of mother unknown or child not living with mother (weighted) n=5428	33.30	19.96	15.96	14.93	27.04	30.91	33.99	16.74
Total number of cases in unweighted sample	5824	5709	5766	6990	1527	3171	3009	16317

TABLE 4.A.2 Regressions on student grades composite by public school and Catholic school

Variable	Public school standardized coefficient	Catholic school standardized coefficient
Parents' highest education	.067***	.043*
Family income	.061***	-.017
Asian	.046***	.032
Hispanic	.049***	-.047**
African American	.084***	.057**
Urban	-.045***	-.039
Suburban	-.054***	.010
Sex of student (male=1, female=0)	-.078***	-.055**
Mother, stepfather	-.035***	-.037
Single mother	-.045***	-.044*
Part-time	.0556	.036
Not in labor force	.021**	.029
Mother's age	-.009	.013
Number of siblings	-.002	-.034
Achievement test score composite	.494***	.558***
Homework hours per week	.064***	.026
R^2	.320	.356

* $p < .05$; ** $p < .01$; *** $p < .001$

Table 4.A.3 Means, standard deviations, and correlations for regressions

	Par ed	Income	Asian	Hispan	Af Amr	Urban	Suburb	Sex	Steppar	S. mom	Part tm	Nlabfrc	M. age	Sibs
Mean	3.071	9.816	0.033	0.092	0.112	0.235	0.444	0.499	0.119	0.150	0.198	0.227	39.849	1.512
Standard deviation	0.954	1.937	0.144	0.233	0.254	0.342	0.401	0.404	0.262	0.288	0.322	0.338	4.611	1.013
Sample n	18854	18066	18675	18675	18675	18861	18861	18861	18685	18685	18861	18861	18499	18858
Parents' highest ed.	1.000													
Family income	0.506	1.000												
Asian	0.082	0.033	1.000											
Hispanic	-0.181	-0.168	-0.059	1.000										
African American	-0.108	-0.236	-0.065	-0.113	1.000									
Urban	0.004	-0.067	0.037	0.116	0.218	1.000								
Suburban	0.109	0.184	0.037	-0.031	-0.117	-0.496	1.000							
Sex of student (male=1)	0.008	0.028	0.009	0.001	-0.006	0.005	-0.007	1.000						
Mother, stepfather	-0.055	-0.044	-0.034	-0.006	0.034	0.002	0.001	-0.030	1.000					
Single mother	-0.135	-0.380	-0.040	0.009	0.194	0.085	-0.050	-0.018	-0.155	1.000				
Mother employed part time	0.082	0.043	-0.015	-0.040	-0.062	-0.027	0.042	-0.005	-0.053	-0.082	1.000			
Mother not in labor force	-0.053	-0.054	-0.006	0.059	-0.080	-0.009	0.003	-0.005	-0.015	-0.115	-0.269	1.000		
Mother's age	0.155	0.134	0.056	0.009	-0.089	0.009	0.065	0.039	-0.183	-0.024	0.031	0.042	1.000	
Number of siblings	-0.065	-0.065	0.024	0.110	0.021	0.021	-0.003	-0.015	-0.002	-0.079	0.014	0.164	-0.060	1.000
Talk abt current school exper	0.214	0.175	-0.029	-0.070	-0.045	-0.028	0.022	-0.104	-0.013	-0.049	0.042	-0.013	0.019	-0.049
Talk abt high schl program	0.125	0.089	-0.002	-0.011	0.032	0.027	0.028	-0.031	-0.021	0.011	0.028	-0.013	0.018	-0.053
Frequency parents restrict tv	0.161	0.073	0.074	0.044	-0.009	0.037	0.030	0.008	-0.035	-0.052	0.050	0.035	0.028	0.083
After school supervision	0.026	0.017	0.002	0.018	-0.035	0.001	-0.006	-0.007	-0.052	-0.092	0.028	0.155	0.034	0.068
Extra music class	0.298	0.225	0.037	-0.082	-0.064	-0.009	0.056	-0.119	-0.067	-0.044	0.055	-0.023	0.128	-0.043
Friends' parents known	0.224	0.234	-0.085	-0.134	-0.142	-0.099	-0.003	-0.031	-0.065	-0.078	0.079	-0.012	0.096	-0.082
Frequ parents contact school	0.155	0.113	-0.032	0.002	0.008	0.041	0.026	0.122	-0.001	-0.016	0.017	-0.037	0.019	-0.020
PTO participation	0.249	0.227	-0.005	-0.043	0.041	0.091	0.035	0.012	-0.065	-0.065	0.042	0.005	0.101	0.010
Parent volunteers at schl	0.151	0.156	-0.023	-0.039	-0.054	0.028	0.013	-0.011	-0.062	-0.077	0.073	0.080	0.080	0.025
Catholic	0.075	0.089	0.003	0.001	-0.022	0.162	0.015	-0.003	0.014	0.008	0.017	0.092	0.022	0.205
Other religious	0.118	0.096	0.016	-0.039	-0.044	0.091	0.008	0.000	0.087	0.040	0.090	0.072	0.040	0.125
Secular private	0.146	0.124	0.025	-0.029	-0.030	0.087	-0.055	0.008	0.026	0.032	0.058	0.059	0.016	0.080
Grades	0.289	0.251	0.068	-0.070	-0.083	-0.037	0.030	-0.102	-0.060	-0.105	0.046	0.006	0.065	-0.022
Test scores	0.401	0.350	0.049	-0.147	-0.236	-0.068	0.093	-0.053	-0.055	-0.088	0.073	-0.018	0.107	-0.048
Homework hours per week	0.401	0.350	0.049	0.047	-0.236	-0.068	0.093	-0.052	-0.019	-0.024	0.022	0.005	0.064	-0.007

(continues)

Table 4.A.3 (continued)

	Cur talk	Talk hs	Restr tv	Superv	Music	Friends	Contact	PTO	Volunt	Cathlc	O relig	Secpriv	Grades	Test scr	Homwk
Mean	1.463	1.308	1.153	-1.811	0.261	2.784	1.102	0.963	0.197	0.077	0.030	0.016	2.933	50.869	4.110
Standard deviation	0.435	0.496	0.858	0.971	0.355	1.324	0.957	0.904	0.321	0.215	0.138	0.102	0.605	8.016	1.184
Sample n	18533	18339	18718	18522	17644	18111	17978	18339	18076	18861	18861	18861	18677	18267	17711
Talk abt currnt schl exper	1.000														
Talk abt high schl prgram	0.329	1.000													
Frequ parents restrict tv	0.172	0.117	1.000												
After schl supervision	0.062	0.035	0.091	1.000											
Extra music class	0.153	0.091	0.122	0.041	1.000										
Friends' parents known	0.178	0.079	0.017	0.033	0.166	1.000									
Frequ parents contct schl	0.027	0.049	0.073	-0.018	0.089	0.089	1.000								
PTO participation	0.113	0.090	0.094	0.047	0.188	0.224	0.193	1.000							
Parent volunteers at schl	0.101	0.062	0.065	0.056	0.141	0.192	0.132	0.396	1.000						
Catholic	0.030	0.012	0.014	0.008	0.017	0.092	0.022	0.205	0.249	1.000					
Other religious	0.059	0.006	0.087	0.040	0.090	0.072	0.040	0.125	0.120	-0.051	1.000				
Secular private	0.037	0.007	0.026	0.032	0.058	0.059	0.016	0.080	0.093	-.0370	-0.022	1.000			
Grades	0.284	0.182	0.107	0.108	0.209	0.189	-0.107	0.166	0.114	0.064	0.059	0.038	1.000		
Test scores	0.285	0.127	0.121	0.085	0.252	0.206	-0.053	0.137	0.106	0.070	0.087	0.082	0.545	1.000	
Homework (hours per wk)	0.206	0.156	0.151	0.025	0.093	0.076	0.011	0.083	0.081	0.065	0.036	0.061	0.178	0.203	1.000

5

Parental Intervention in the School: The Context of Minority Involvement

David Kerbow and Annette Bernhardt

The educational literature has demonstrated that children's academic success is highly associated with family background. While the mechanisms are complex, this link of family background to academic achievement is at least partially tied to parents' engagement with their child's education: both with the child directly and through the school (Baker and Stevenson 1986; Lareau 1987, 1989; Marjoribanks 1979; Stevenson and Baker 1987; Teachman 1987). Arguments for the benefits of parental involvement often enter into discussions of academically disadvantaged students. Children from economically or educationally disadvantaged families face a number of ill-defined obstacles in the learning process; consequently, they may depend more than usual on support from their parents.

Parental involvement would therefore seem to be especially critical for certain minority groups. African American and Hispanic families in particular are disproportionately represented in the lower socioeconomic groups, and their children tend to have lower grades and standardized test scores. Recent policy initiatives have supported programs designed to increase minority parent engagement with the education of their child (Berger 1991; Brandt 1979; Landerholm 1988). An underlying assumption of such policy implementation is that levels of parental involvement for these parents are inadequate or at least below expected levels and, thus, contribute to the deficit of lower social class background.

A less explicit supposition about the process of parental involvement is that it originates and is contained within the family. Involvement is seen as primarily, if not exclusively, a matter of motivation. Motivated parents value education, which may be seen either as an avenue for the improvement of the child's life chances or as an inherent good for the enhancement of the child's life. Given realistic constraints on their time and financial resources, such parents will devote energy to their child's educational achievement.

Undoubtedly, parents' interest in the education of their child plays a role, but other factors also affect this individual-level process. As a dominant presence in the everyday life of each student, the school clearly influences the extent that parents intervene in or manage their child's formal education. Schools can present formidable barriers to such involvement; as professional institutions, they may devote themselves mainly to providing educational services and indirectly maintain relationships with parents which are on the periphery. On the other hand, school structures can be inclusive of individual parents and the parent community. Teachers may interact more frequently with parents and, as a consequence, encourage reciprocal contact. Unfortunately, this larger context of school practices is quite often neglected in discussions of what parents can do to help their child's education (for a theoretical discussion, see Epstein 1987; Litwak and Meyer 1974; for empirical research, see Hoover-Dempsey et al. 1987; Van Galen 1987).

Thus, four factors may be suggested that affect the extent that parents participate in the process of educating their children. First, parents may or may not have the *motivation* to be involved because of the possible benefits education might bring. These expectations (or lack of expectations) about future opportunities may drive their actions. Second, financial and other educational *resources* of the parents may facilitate or restrict the extent of involvement they choose. Parents with limited education themselves may have less expertise or information about how to intervene in their child's education. Third, parents may face *time constraints* which foreclose the possibility of some forms of involvement. Afternoon activities may not be feasible for working parents. Finally, *school policies* or other characteristics of the school may hinder or encourage involvement. Parents who have similar approaches to educating their child may have strikingly different patterns of involvement because of the school their child attends.

This chapter takes a closer look at these factors and the assumptions commonly associated with them. Although the assumptions appear to be quite plausible, our analysis suggests that they can be seriously misleading if viewed too narrowly. Involvement is a contextual process; it is shaped by both school-level as well as individual-level factors. Our research yields an understanding of parental involvement as problematic, in that parents face constraints on their involvement. It is significantly affected by lack of resources within the family and is shaped in important ways by the environment the school provides.

The primary focus of our analysis is on African American and Hispanic parents, since policy discussion tends to gravitate toward these groups. These families, in addition to being of lower socioeconomic status, experience school settings which are quite different from those experienced by their majority counterparts. Consequently, the possible effect of school context on involvement becomes especially important. This context may be crucial not only for the shaping of involvement but also for understanding the outcome of parental involvement as well — that is, the effect on student performance.

This chapter has five sections. The first discusses the various forms of parental participation in more detail, providing a description of the variables which were constructed as well as basic statistics about the prevalence of involvement among parents. Special attention is given to school-related activities. The next section presents a brief outline of the methodological techniques which are employed. Considering school-level factors requires statistical procedures which directly model their effects. The third section, which begins the analytical part of the chapter, addresses the issues of involvement from the perspective of the individual parent. The discussion in the fourth section brings in the school as a potential factor in choices about involvement. The fifth section, then, offers a two part explanation of the potential school effect which deals, first, with the racial composition of the schools and, second, with particular policies and school characteristics. The conclusion provides a brief summary as well as preliminary policy implications.

Forms of Parental Involvement

Engagement of parents with the academic experience of their children takes place along a number of dimensions. Perhaps the most basic level of involvement is within the home. Parents convey expectations and set priorities for their children through their everyday interaction. Their involvement, such as talking with the child about school experiences or future goals, may be explicitly focused toward educational achievement as well. Other forms of involvement incorporate additional actors into the process. The school and its personnel may be viewed by the parent as a resource for information or as an avenue of success for the child. Even though the parent may be comfortable discussing educational plans with the child, he or she may not readily contact the school because of uneasiness about speaking to teachers or, alternatively, because avenues of contact are not clearly provided. Parental involvement will be shaped by different aspects of the school as well as by different characteristics of the parent.

We have developed variables which correspond to these differing forms of engagement. Although parents have interests in their child's education independent of the school, these interests may not straightforwardly translate into contact with teachers and staff. The school will mediate this translation. And, in fact, the effectiveness of home-based involvement in promoting educational goals and achievement may be dependent on these forms of interaction with the school.[1] Therefore, while taking into account the parents' level of activity in the home, we focus on two forms of parental involvement with the school: (1) parent-initiated contact with the school about academic matters, and (2) participation in parent-teacher organizations at the school.[2]

Parent contact with the school about their child's academic progress or program is an immediate form of engagement. Overall, approximately 53% of the parents said they had contacted the school about their child's academic performance at least once since school opened. Fewer parents (35%) said they had contacted the school about their children's academic programs over the same period. These actions can constitute a type of crisis intervention, as when the child is not performing at expected levels. Contact in this instance is an attempt to marshal the resources of the school to address the specific needs of the child at that moment. Alternatively, contact when a student is performing well may indicate an attempt to enhance the educational resources available to the child, for example, by asking about advanced courses. Whichever scenario is applicable, this directed action is likely to be a response to the child's performance. Therefore, considering an indicator such as the student's grades will be important.

Formal involvement with the school through participation in parent-teacher groups constitutes, on the other hand, a more diffuse type of engagement. Approximately 32% of the parents stated that they belonged to such an organization, while 36% said they attended meetings. These activities are much less tied to the immediate, day-to-day performance of the child, although a long-term interest in that performance is clearly present. Decisions on school policy may be dealt with in these groups; extracurricular activities for students may be planned; or, school fund raising may be discussed. Each of these areas will ultimately affect the children's educational environment. It is likely, then, that parental participation will be influenced by how far a parent expects his or her child to go in school. Thus, we will include parents' educational expectations when modeling this type of involvement.[3]

Methodological Considerations

Two statistical techniques are employed in the analysis. Standard ordinary least squares (OLS) is utilized initially to consider individual-level factors and characteristics of parents which might affect involvement. In this analysis, parents are considered as one group; their participation in different schools with varying practices toward parents is not entertained. The OLS estimates, in this context, are actually combinations of both individual and school level influences. Unfortunately, with OLS analysis, it is not possible to parse out the contribution of individual as opposed to schools effects. Even contextual analysis, the conventional approach to modeling school-level characteristics in OLS regression, does not sufficiently address this potential problem (Burstein 1980). Unless the school-level variables that are modeled in the contextual analysis completely account for the between school variation, the individual-level coefficients will continue to be biased.

The most adequate method for addressing such questions is hierarchical linear modeling (Bryk and Raudenbush 1992; Mason, Wong, and Entwistle 1983). HLM relies on equations that correspond to the two levels of analysis. At the individual or parent level, involvement is predicted within each school. Thus, the estimated coefficients are not influenced at this stage by differing school contexts; the context is the same for parents in the same school. At the second level, the mean involvement in the school is modeled. In addition, the variability (across schools) of individual level relationships is modeled separately. This method allows identification and separation of two distinct processes: (1) relationships at the individual level which hold within the schools; and (2) differences between schools which either offset or accentuate individual-level relationships.[4]

The Individual-Level Context

The shaping of the process of parental involvement is complicated when the multiplicity of actors and contexts is considered. We simplify the problem by initially addressing the individual level: the influence of characteristics of parents and their children, especially their racial/ethnic status, on parental participation. With this background, the focus will then shift to examining how the school affects these individual relationships.

When a parent becomes involved in the child's education, two sets of individual-level factors potentially play a role. The first set centers around attitudes and values about education. This aspect is tapped by parents' expectations for the child's future educational attainment, expressed values about the school and the schooling process, and parental confidence in the school. Equally important is a second set of factors — the realm of resources. Even if a parent is motivated to participate in her child's education, she may be constrained by an inflexible work schedule, limited education, financial pressures, or the absence of a spouse. Both sets of factors certainly exert influence over a parent's behavior; their interplay and relative importance, however, is crucial in formulating school policies to enhance parent engagement.

Table 5.1 contains strictly individual-level estimates (OLS) of the two forms of parental involvement: contacting the school about the child's academic performance or academic program and participation in a parent-teacher organization. As anticipated, families of higher socioeconomic status display significantly higher rates of both types of involvement—the role of family resources is clearly indicated here. Other resource-related variables (not shown here) such as family work schedules, number of parents present in the home, and number of siblings also exert influence. And while high parental expectations for the child's future education also have an impact on balance, the direct effect of resources clearly outweighs the values or motivational aspects of parental involvement. Thus, it appears that while many parents begin with the desire to help their child's education in some way, the translation of this desire into action is much more difficult for lower-class parents.

TABLE 5.1 Individual-level models of parental involvement—OLS regression

	Forms of parental involvement	
	Academic contacts	PTO participation
Socioeconomic status	.360***	.343***
Student's grades	-.312***	.050***
Parents' educational expectations	.014*	.070***
Race/ethnicity		
African American	.185***	.310***
Hispanic	.168***	.059***
Asian	-.172***	-.127**
African American grades	.219***	.139***
R^2	7.7%	11.3%

* = significant at .05 level; ** = significant at .01 level; *** = significant at .001 level

Note: Both models are adjusted for student's sex, parent's working status, family composition, number of children in the family, extent of educational discussion in the home, and directed educational discussion in the home.

As anticipated, the student's grades also play a prominent role in parent-initiated contact with the school. Parents of students who are not performing well have more contacts, presumably seeking information and guidance. We thus have evidence that this type of involvement is usually an act of "crisis intervention." The relationship between grades and formal participation in the school, however, goes in the opposite direction: such participation is greater by parents of students who perform well. Since parent-teacher organizations are not child-specific, we would anticipate less association with the immediate performance of the child. In fact, parental expectations have a more significant effect. PTO participation provides parents with access to the decision making body of the school. Parents desiring information about the broader schooling process and hoping to influence its long-term policy utilize the PTO as a means of access. Consequently, those with more interest in their child's educational future tend to include this form of involvement along with other types of participation.

But perhaps the most striking result from these models is the following: *African Americans and Hispanics show significantly more involvement with their child's school than white or Asian parents of the same socioeconomic background.* These differences prove to be extremely robust. Even when other factors such as family structure, parents' working status, or number of siblings are controlled for, the positive gap between minority and white participation remains. (See Fehrmann, Keith, and Reimers 1987 for comparable results in secondary school.)

Asian parents in particular have notably lower involvement with the school concerning their children's education. It should be noted, however, that in other areas, such as visiting museums and enrolling their children in music or other classes, Asian parents are higher than other groups. Thus, their patterns of involvement are quite different from those of other minority or white parents. School-related involvement is only one aspect of engagement with children's education that parents may choose to undertake. Some parental groups access the school as a route to involvement more than others.[5]

Given that African American and Hispanic parents are disproportionately concentrated in the lower classes with fewer resources, the expectation is often that they would display uniformly lower levels of school involvement. In fact, these minority groups tend to offset the detrimental effect of lower resources. To give a tangible illustration of how striking this effect is, we did the following comparison in Table 5.2. The average socioeconomic status is much lower for minorities than for whites. Holding all other variables constant, we substitute these different class background

TABLE 5.2 Predicted parental involvement—socioeconomic and racial/ethnic differences*

	Academic contacts			PTO participation		
	African American	Hispanic	White	African American	Hispanic	White
Predicted involvement based on socioeco-nomic differences	.820	.836	1.027	.828	.8441	.025
Actual involvement of parents	.970	.991	1.027	1.138	.900	1.025
Percentage of socio-economic disadvantage offset by minority parents	73%	82%	-	157%	31%	-

*Predictions are based on estimates from models in Table 1. These predictions hold characterictics of the parents constant except for socioeconomic status of the racial/ethnic groups in the first prediction (row 1) and the race/ethnicity of the parent as well as the socioeconomic status in the second prediction (row 2).

Note: The average socioeconomic status measures of the racial/ethnic groups are: African American -.501; Hispanic -.455; White .074.

levels into the equations. The result is a predicted involvement level for each racial/ethnic group, assuming that race/ethnicity has no effect. That is, we assume that the only effect of race is related to differences in socioeconomic status between the groups. The predicted amount of contact with the school would be .820 for the average African American parent; for the average Hispanic parent, .836; for the average white parent, 1.027. There is, then, an expected gap of .206 between African American and white parents. But the actual gap between white and African American parents in their school contacts is only .056. Thus, these parents manage to offset over 73% of the detrimental effect of their disadvantaged background. And Hispanic parents offset 82% of this disadvantage.

Similar results hold for levels of participation in parent-teacher organizations. African American parents are actually able to more than compensate for their lower class status. This means that they engage the school through formal organizations more frequently than white parents, even though they are of lower socioeconomic status. Hispanic parents in this form of involvement also reduce the anticipated gap due to their class background, by 31%.

Last, we have a final indication that African American parents more intensely access the school in their concern about their child's education. Recall in Table 5.1 that most parents contact the school considerably less if the student is bringing home good grades. African American parents, however, continue to initiate contact even when their child's grades are relatively high (the grade effect for this group is less pronounced). These parents intervene when the student is in crisis, as do others, but in addition they also contact the school frequently even when their child is receiving relatively high grades. Similarly, recall that parents whose child has good grades will tend to participate in formal organizations of the school. This effect is much more pronounced for African American parents. The increase in their involvement with increase in child's grades is almost three times the rate of other groups.

Bringing in the School Context

At this point, having only considered individual-level factors, we cannot yet explain why minority parents show more involvement with their children than white parents. But these two types of parental involvement entail considerable interaction with the school. Moreover, minorities tend to be concentrated in very different schools than whites: African American and Hispanic students more often attend schools with low average socio-economic status, in urban areas, with very high concentrations of their racial or ethnic group.

Thus, we should consider the possibility that the school context is having a significant effect on the parental involvement process and especially on differing levels of involvement between minority and white parents. The above models treat all parents and their children as one group. The comparison was between parents who have similar characteristics without respect to the school their children attend. Therefore, perhaps a more appropriate comparison would be between parents within the same school. How parents interact with each other obviously depends on the type of parents in the school, as well as the school's structures for facilitating such interaction. For example, in one school, contacting administrative staff or reaching a child's teacher may be uncomplicated even when the parent has a demanding work schedule, but in another school productive contact may not be feasible without taking a day off. A parent's wishes for the child's program placement may be routinely incorporated in the decision making process in one context, but ignored in another. A teacher or counselor may decide to deal with a student's problem by drawing on a host of school programs and services, or the family may be brought in from the outset as the preferred avenue of recourse.

These stylized examples are meant to convey the variety of ways a school can influence what and how much parents do to aid their child's education. Ignoring the possibility of such an influence, as we did in the analyses above, may seriously hamper our understanding of parental involvement. Not only could we overlook important influences that have strong policy implications, we could also develop a distorted picture of those factors that are considered.

School effects can make themselves felt in two distinct ways. First, different schools might show very different average levels of parental involvement. Since these schools probably also differ on characteristics such as class background, geographic location, or racial composition, a strictly individual-level model will incorporate these average differences, but their precise influence on the individual relationships will be unclear and in some sense misleading. Second, not only might the school influence the participation of all parents, it may also have differing effects on parents with different backgrounds. A parent's race, full-time working status, socioeconomic background, or language ability may matter in some schools more than in others. In our context, if indeed the individual characteristics of parents fully explain their involvement (implying that the school context has no significant effect), then, adjusting for the effects of socioeconomic status, minority parents should participate at the same higher rate in each school, regardless of the type of school in question.

This is not, however, the case. Table 5.3 provides re-estimations of the individual involvement *within schools*. Before considering specific variables, first notice that the between-school variation is significant in both models. Differences between schools account for 5% of the extent to which parents contact the school about their child's academic standing. These differences have a markedly stronger effect on how much parents participate formally in the school, accounting for 18.5% of the variation. That the school effect would differ for the two types of parental involvement seems quite plausible. As argued above, parent contact with the school is often an act of crisis intervention; for example, when the student's grades are falling. Given the implied urgency, the school is likely to have less effect on whether the parent takes action. If we turn to participation in parent-teacher organizations, however, the role of the school is clearly present; the effectiveness of the PTO, its composition and structure, the extent to which it is publicized, its political outlook, all may affect whether a parent attends.

School context, then, clearly plays an important role. We now consider the separate variables and their within school re-estimations. Notice that for both types of parental involvement, the standard variables in the models (socioeconomic status, grades, parents' educational expectations) show roughly the same associations with involvement as they did in Table 5.1.[6]

It is rather the racial/ethnic differences that undergo striking changes. Let us first examine how much parents contact the school about their child's academic progress. Although the two minority variables remain significant and positive, they have weakened considerably from the strictly indi-

TABLE 5.3 Within school individual-level models of parental involvement—hierarchical linear models

	Forms of parental involvement	
	Academic contacts	PTO participation
Socioeconomic status	.323***	.259***
Student's grades	-.299***	.068***
Parents' educational expectations	.017*	.053***
Race/ethnicity		
African American	.090*	.014
Hispanic	.081*	-.057
Asian	-.118*	-.263***
African American grades	.154***	.052*
Between school variation	5.0%	18.5%

* = significant at .05 level; ** = significant at .01 level; *** = significant at .001 level

Note: Both models are adjusted for student's sex, parent's working status, family composition, number of children in the family, extent of educational discussion in the home, and directed educational discussion in the home.

vidual-level model by approximately 50%. Close to half of the higher minority involvement rate is due to the school context which the parent confronts. Thus in general, controlling for socioeconomic background, minority parents contact the school more often than their white counterparts. However, if we make the comparison within schools only, the difference, while still substantial, is reduced by one-half. As we will see, this result obtains because minority parents tend to be concentrated in schools that have higher rates of parental contact overall.

This dynamic is much stronger in the model of participation in formal school organizations. The African American and Hispanic coefficients actually become *insignificant.* Under the strictly individual-level estimation, when the comparison was across the population of parents, the race effect was second in strength, only to that of socioeconomic status. When comparisons are made within schools, however, the estimated gap between white, African American, and Hispanic parent participation disappears. Once we account for the fact that the three racial/ethnic groups are located in schools which differ on a number of dimensions, then there remain no significant differences between the groups' rate of involvement. Within any given school, these three sets of parents are involved in PTO organizations at similar rates (although Asian parents are involved at a lower rate); but, as we will see, African Americans and Hispanics tend to be situated in schools that have more active parent-teacher organizations as a whole.

Explaining the School Effect—Part I

At this point, there is compelling evidence of a school effect. But let us be clear. This effect does not negate our earlier finding that minority parents are more involved in their child's school than white parents of the same social class. Rather, we suggest that a critical link to this process lies with the types of schools in which African Americans and Hispanics tend to be situated: schools that have significantly higher rates of parental involvement overall.

The question that immediately arises, of course, is what the characteristics of this "school context" are. The possible school characteristics that could be hypothesized to affect parents' participation is large. Because our interest is primarily with racial/ethnic differences, we first focus on one straightforward but quite interesting property: the concentration of minority students. Middle schools in the United States exhibit a high degree of segregation among racial/ethnic groups. More than half of African American students attend schools in which they are the predominant (40% or higher) group; 42% of Hispanics attend schools with high concentrations (over 50%) of Hispanic students. And 60% of white students attend schools in which they are overwhelmingly the majority (90% or higher).

What impact does this concentration of minority students within schools have on parental activity? Table 5.4 provides HLM models which address this question. First notice that in both models, the average socioeconomic status in the school increases the extent to which parents participate in their child's education. This is as one might expect, since social class is in general a strong predictive factor.

More interesting is that *once average socioeconomic background is taken into account, schools with very high concentrations of African American and Hispanic students show significantly higher levels of both types of parental involvement.* The strength of this effect is quite compelling. And these higher levels of parental involvement are confirmed by administrators' reports from the same schools (also see Erbe et al. 1990 for corroborating results in Chicago Public Schools). We introduced a number of control variables which might render this relationship spurious, among them differences between school sectors (Catholic, private, public), school location (urban, rural, suburban), and school size. The relationship, however, continued to be strongly significant.

Why the presence of other minorities has an impact only after a critical threshold is reached is an interesting question.[7] At this point we can only speculate. One possibility is that these high concentration schools are located in cohesive, minority communities that center around ethnic or

TABLE 5.4 School-level parental involvement and school racial/ethnic composition—hierarchical linear models

| | School-level parental involvement | |
	Academic contacts	PTO participation
Average school socioeconomic status	.299***	.696***
Racial/ethnic composition[†]		
More than 41% African American	.165***	.289***
More than 51% Hispanic	.127*	.283***
R^2	16.9%	33.1%

* = significant at .05 level; ** = significant at .01 level; *** = significant at .001 level

†Other models of the effect of minority composition of schools were also developed. In particular, a linear and quadratic variable for the percentage of African American and Hispanic students were included. These variables revealed similar findings. Parental involvement was higher in predominately minority schools.

racial identification. It is likely that there is a spill-over effect whereby interaction between the school and the community is facilitated. Another related explanation would suggest that within these schools there is less of a possibility for conflict along racial lines. Especially since these schools tend to have more minority teachers (as we will discuss), parents may feel more comfortable calling a teacher, raising criticisms of school policy, or insisting on a program placement for their child.

What is impressive is that these high concentration schools have overwhelmingly disadvantaged constituents. Fully 85% of the Hispanic schools and 63% of the African American schools have an average socioeconomic status that is in the lowest quartile (compared to 13% of predominately white schools in the lowest quartile). The majority of these schools are large public schools, located in urban areas, with average test scores predominantly in the lowest quartile of the national distribution.[8] And yet, parental activity in these schools is comparatively high.

Figure 5.1 illustrates these differences in levels of involvement. We first defined schools with low, moderate, and high average socioeconomic levels. Within these groups, we then separated schools that had high concentrations of the three racial/ethnic groups. As is evident in both charts, strong minority presence in a school can significantly help to offset the detrimental effect that low average socioeconomic status usually has on parental involvement. In fact, these schools display levels of parental involvement approaching that of high socioeconomic status, largely white schools.

FIGURE 5.1 (two parts)

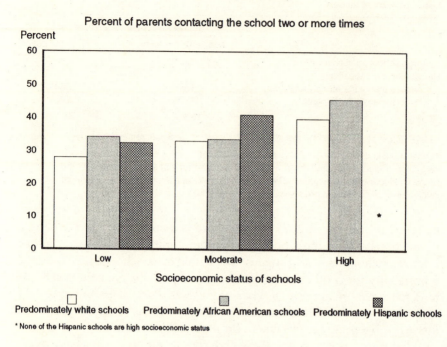

Percent of parents contacting the school two or more times

* None of the Hispanic schools are high socioeconomic status

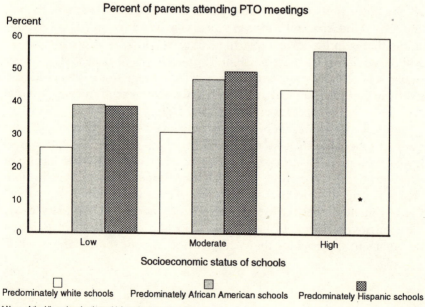

Percent of parents attending PTO meetings

* None of the Hispanic schools are high socioeconomic status

Explaining the School Effect—Part II

Why do these schools with a largely minority population foster parental involvement, when their generally lower-class composition would predict otherwise? While a number of factors might be at work (e.g., community or cultural characteristics) we limit our attention to school-specific influences.

In the following section, three important properties of schools are considered. First are characteristics of the teaching staff: the racial composition of teachers and the extent of teacher- and school-initiated interaction with parents and their children. Second is how the school invests in the long-term educational welfare of the students; specifically, whether it guides the students through the transition to high school. Third are indications of how much the school presses the students toward academic progress through explicit, rather than informal, policies and practices.

Recall that the first form of involvement, the extent to which parents contact the school about their child's academic progress and program placement, is a specific type of engagement; the contact is usually one-on-one, most often with a teacher. The issue is specific to the parent's own child. Often, the reason for the contact is pressing—the child's academic performance is below a particular level. Other times, the parent contacts out of his or her own initiative, concerned about the particular program or trajectory of the child. Since this contact is focused and immediate, we expect that equally immediate school properties—those entailing direct interaction—will have the most noticeable impact.

Table 5.5 confirms this expectation. Of the three forms of school variables discussed above, only the characteristics and practices of the teaching staff show a significant effect.[9] Clearly, the more teachers and school staff contact the parents specifically about their children, the more they encourage reciprocal contacts initiated by the parents. (See Becker and Epstein [1982] and Epstein and Becker [1982] for a discussion of teacher practices that incorporate parents into the educational process; see also Powell 1978.) A strong feedback relationship is quite evident. We also see more parental contact when the proportion of minority teachers increases.[10]

The critical point is that these variables reduce the estimated African American and Hispanic school effects. The actions and characteristics of teachers at these schools contribute to the explanation of the higher levels of parental contact. One aspect associated with higher contact is that many of the teachers in the minority schools are also minorities. In largely African American schools, roughly half of the teachers are of the same race; in largely Hispanic schools, a third are of the same ethnicity. In largely white

TABLE 5.5 School-level parental contact about the child's academic progress—hierarchical linear model

	Academic contacts
Average school socioeconomic status	.241***
Racial/ethnic composition†	
More than 41% African American	-.051
More than 51% Hispanic	-.019
Hours/week teachers spend contacting parents	.053*
Proportion of parents contacted by school 3 or more times about students' academic program	3.539***
Proportion of teachers that are African American	.362***
R^2	33.5%

* = significant at .05 level; ** = significant at .01 level; *** = significant at .001 level

†The results of the analysis do not change significantly when linear and quadratic terms are included for minority composition. The estimate for "proportion of teachers that are African American" continues to be highly significant and the effect of school racial composition variables are reduced (although they continues to be marginally significant).

schools the proportion of minority teachers is generally small; minority parents interact primarily with white teachers in those schools. Whatever the specific explanation, such as cultural identification or less perceived prejudgment from teachers, minority parents are more likely to initiate contact in schools where a higher proportion of the teachers is of the same racial/ethnic status.[11]

In addition, parental contact in the minority schools is also heightened because teachers and other school staff spend more of their time interacting with the parent about a number of issues concerning the child. For example, teachers in these minority schools spend roughly 60% more time contacting and talking with parents, as compared to similar white schools. In all likelihood, parent-school contact becomes a reciprocal and ongoing relationship.[12]

When we consider the second measure of involvement, how much parents participate in formal organizations such as PTO, the scope of parental activity becomes much broader. It is not child-specific. The parent's interest is focused more on general school issues and policies, the education process of all the students, the level of institutional decision making. We therefore expect that each set of the school properties will show an effect, since they capture a diverse number of institutional structures.

Table 5.6 presents two models for this type of parental involvement.[13] The first model contains teacher variables quite similar to the ones previously presented, and we again see the same pattern as above—the effects are strong and significant, and reduce the effect of African American and Hispanic schools. Thus, the combined attributes of teacher-initiated contact as well as the resource of a minority teaching staff contribute to the development of activity in parent-teacher organizations. This is especially true for the African American school effect. The percentage of African American teachers, in fact, accounts for 60% of the reduction in the African American schools coefficient. The Hispanic schools display similar if less pronounced trends, although we are unable to directly analyze the effect of predominately Hispanic teaching staffs.

A general conclusion, then, is that how much time and energy teachers put into communication as well as their racial composition does much to encourage both types of parental involvement, and begins to explain why

TABLE 5.6 School-level parent-teacher organization participation—hierarchical linear models

	PTO participation	
	Model 1	Model 2
Average school socioeconomic status	.677***	.631***
Racial/ethnic composition†		
More than 41% African American	.088	.207***
More than 51% Hispanic	.208*	.156*
Hours/week teachers spend contacting parents	.130***	-
Proportion of parents contacted by school 3 or more time about students' academic program	1.130*	-
Proportion of parents who receive information frequently from teachers	.023**	-
Proportion of teachers that are African American	.361*	-
Proportion of students who talk to teacher or guidance counsellor about high school	-	.086***
Standardized tests are employed to assign students to high school courses	-	.086**
Regularity of scheduled period to discuss academic improvement strategies with students	-	.017*
School policy on frequency of homework assignments	-	.100**
Presence of academic press in the school	-	.116***
R^2	37.2%	39.1%

* = significant at .05 level; ** = significant at .01 level; *** = significant at .001 level

†The results are consistent with those above when linear and quadratic terms are employed for schools' racial composition instead of dummy variables. The estimate of "proportion of teachers that are African American" continues to be significant at the .05 level.

minority schools eclipse similarly situated white schools on this account. We therefore seem to be witnessing an interactive process in the African American and Hispanic schools in which an active school staff helps to encourage levels of parental activity.

A potential alternate explanation to this conclusion is important to consider. It could be argued that the heightened levels of contact in minority schools are associated with behavioral problems of the students that require the parents to communicate with the school in some form. In regard to parent-teacher organizations, parental involvement might be a response to concerns about safety in the school. If this general explanation were accurate, the "meaning" of involvement would be quite different in these schools. Although this alternative may initially sound plausible, several observations tend to rule it out as a viable interpretation. First, the previous individual-level models demonstrated that African American parents contact the school frequently even when their children are performing well. Students who are performing well academically are not likely to simultaneously exhibit behavioral problems. Second, inclusion of other variables attempting to measure student behavioral problems (such as absenteeism, frequency of being sent to the principal's office, etc.) did not affect the results. And, finally, higher teacher contact in minority schools also contributes to explaining why parents become more involved in school policy and decision making—an activity much less focused on the individual student. Thus, we conclude that student behavior (or misbehavior) is not the driving force which induces involvement in minority schools.

Therefore, characteristics of the teaching staff clearly influence the level of parental involvement. But what about the other two types of school properties? The second model in Table 5.6 presents their effects on formal parental involvement. The first group of variables captures an aspect of the school's commitment to the long-term educational welfare of the students, by explicitly guiding and overseeing the transition of the student to high school. As we see, these practices are significantly related to higher parental input into formal decision making organizations. Schools which exhibit these characteristics draw both student and parent into a critical part of the educational transition; the parent activity is instituted in part through increased PTO membership and attendance.

The remaining variables give an indication of how the school presses and encourages students toward academic achievement. Schools can accomplish this in a variety of ways (Pink 1987; Sizemore 1987). Some use more informal methods which vary depending on the individual teacher and student, others explicitly require certain practices as a matter of institutional policy, such as a frequency of homework assignments or an atmosphere of academic press.[14] Not surprisingly, policies such as these show a strong and positive association with parental participation in school organizations, and again, we surmise that a feedback process between parental activity and school effort is at work.

The minority schools, in fact, when compared to majority white schools of the same socioeconomic status, display slightly higher levels of the characteristics described above, in particular discussion of academic strategies and an explicit homework policy. As a result, the magnitude of the minority school effect is reduced when these qualities are held constant. Their explanatory force, however, is not pronounced in African American schools when compared to the influence of more direct teacher characteristics. Their influence is slightly more evident in Hispanic schools, with a reduction in the Hispanic school effect of more than 45%. Explicit policies in these schools provide an environment which facilitates parent activity. Thus, in general, we have an indication that structural features of school policy and practice encourage parental involvement in parent-teacher organizations. In addition, these qualities provide some impetus for higher involvement in minority schools.

In sum, we have gained an informative and at times surprising picture about some of the processes at work in schools with large numbers of African American and Hispanic students. Their comparatively higher rates of parental involvement depend at least in part on what the parents and the schools make of their resources. While the parents may bring the initial motivation, it is clear that the schools contribute as well. One potential resource these schools offer is a minority teaching staff. Whatever the social and cultural mechanism, this minority presence on the school's side is associated with more activity by the parents. These schools also rely on their teachers and school staff to contact parents about their child's progress and future placement. We argue that a feedback process is most likely operative: involved parents are more demanding of the school and positive responses from the school encourage further involvement.

It is important to remember that this picture of involvement in the minority schools is favorable only in comparison to white schools of the same social class. Clearly, schools located in disadvantaged areas and with lower class constituents, whatever their race, do not perform academically as well as schools of high socioeconomic status. We believe, however, that our method of comparison is critical. For it suggests that if there is a race difference in parental and teacher activity in disadvantaged schools, it is largely minority schools which hold the advantage in the comparison.

Conclusion

We began by tracing some common assumptions about parental involvement in the education process. Our findings indicate that these assumptions may be too facile when considering this complicated process. The result may be policy directives with misguided priorities.

Specifically, we found that parental involvement is most affected by the presence or absence of family resources: lower class background, full-time working status, one parent in the household, all take their toll on how much the parent is able to accomplish. Thus, while most parents express concern about their children's education, the lack of adequate resources presents a significant obstacle to involvement.

Since minority parents disproportionately confront this obstacle of limited resources, one might expect to find less involvement for African American and Hispanic parents. In fact, we find that these parents manage to compensate, and actually exhibit significantly higher rates of parental involvement compared to white parents of the same social class. We suggest that disadvantaged groups place a higher value on education as the main avenue of economic mobility.[15] If indeed parents from minority groups view education in this manner, one would expect more tenacity as far as actual participation is concerned. That is, while these parents are hampered by very tangible and immediate resource constraints, their orientation toward education reduces the impact of those constraints. To claim that these parents are inadequate in their attention to their children's education is straightforwardly mistaken.

Moreover, when the pivotal role of school context is recognized, we gain additional insight into the complex configuration of minority involvement. The most commanding school characteristic for minority parents and their children is that they are overwhelmingly located in schools that are public, urban, and largely minority in composition. And, counter to some presuppositions, schools with especially high concentrations of minorities show markedly more parental involvement than is evident in comparable white schools. Parents in these schools frequently access the institution about their child's academic progress. They also engage in broader activities that are aimed at improving the general educational environment in the school through formal participation in groups such as parent-teacher organizations.

In part, this involvement is a response to school policies and structures that are inclusive of both parents and students. Teachers and other school staff devote time to communicating with the parents about a number of issues concerning the child. Another attribute, which deserves further attention in future research, is that many more of the teachers are minorities. Either because the potential for conflict is lessened or because initial identification is more immediate, parents in these schools interact with teachers more frequently.

Recently, much energy has been spent on devising policies by which schools serving disadvantaged students draw on internal resources and on their constituents to increase the academic achievement of their students. Policies that have been proposed suggest an ideal scenario where parents are routinely incorporated into the education process, with increased contact between school personnel and parents as well as the formation of a parent group that could lend support to the task of education. In fact, the portrait of largely African American and Hispanic schools which has emerged from the analysis contains at least some elements that conform to this policy initiative.[16]

Nevertheless, standardized measures of academic achievement within minority schools lag significantly behind national averages (by 13% on the NELS: 1988 test). Comparatively, even majority white schools of similar social background display slightly higher standardized scores than their minority counterparts. Preliminary analysis, however, does reveal evidence of more indirect academic effects, which may be related to minority parental involvement. Compared to predominantly white schools of the same social class background, the concentrated minority schools have the following characteristics: the average number of hours of homework students complete during a week is higher, and the gap between minority and white students' grades is considerably reduced and even eliminated in some cases.

Given this description of both standardized and indirect effects, our portrait of predominantly minority schools poses an apparent contradiction. Parents utilize the school on a number of levels to aid their child's education, and the school in fact responds with reciprocated interest by teachers. And yet, a primary measure of academic achievement—standardized test scores—does not seem to be significantly affected.

This incongruity is critical because it indicates that there may be limitations to educational policies centered on these forms of traditional parental involvement. Traditional avenues of involvement with the school such as parent-teacher conferences or PTO membership may not be sufficient for parents to intervene successfully in the education of students who may be "at risk." Additional ties with the school and other external support systems may need to be made available. Such a strategy would expand the role of both the school and the parent.

No matter how active parents may be within the school, a very complex and strong set of factors continues to work against students in disadvantaged contexts. These are parents with very few resources, schools with impoverished families and limited funding. Both confront severe problems that are intimately linked to the communities and environment in which they are located. That they persevere in the face of these problems shows compelling concern for their children. But this effort cannot negate the reality that there is a substantial discrepancy between the resources held by urban schools and their minority parents and those held by affluent suburban schools and their white parents. These resources are not limited to measures of per pupil expenditure. They also relate closely to the presence of community institutions and the social support they provide. Policy research statistically controls for differences in the social class background of students and schools; this necessary research technique, however, should not obscure the fact that these differences often dominate the educational experiences of parents and their students. The translation of parental involvement into student outcomes is not unproblematic: disadvantaged schools in particular may be constrained in their ability to respond adequately to the parent's demands, and therefore, the ultimate effectiveness of parental involvement itself may be reduced.

This analysis suggests that policy focused on motivating disadvantaged minority parents to become involved in their child's education, when they are doing so more than similarly situated white parents, results in a distorted perspective. This does not imply that parental involvement programs do not provide important links between parents and schools; but these initiatives may be misguided if additional attention is not given to the context of constraints which parents and schools face. Questions about how involvement of parents is translated into academic achievement within the school must be addressed, in particular, when the school serves a disadvantaged student body.

Notes

1. While our main concern is with school-related parental activity, we feel that it is important to control for the parent's engagement with the child at home (as measured by frequency of discussions with the child about (1) school experiences and course work and (2) future high school program). The following models are controlled for these measures, although we do not explore them directly. See Chapter 2 for a fuller discussion of home involvement and its context.

2. These two variables have been extensively refined over the course of the project by a number of researchers and are quite robust. Our measure of parental contact with the school combines the number of times the parent contacted the school about (1) the child's academic progress and (2) the child's academic program. Our measure of formal participation in school organizations combines reports as to whether the parent (1) is a member of the PTO; (2) has attended PTO meetings; and (3) participated in PTO activities.

3. A complete description of all variables employed in the paper as well as their means, standard deviations, and correlations are provided in Appendix 5.1.

4. See Appendix 5.2 for a more technical discussion of these issues.

5. In this chapter, we do not focus on Asian involvement. While the comparisons presented on the individual-level are reasonable, the small sample size for this group makes estimation of school-level processes imprecise.

6. Some reduction in estimates is expected in HLM reestimation of OLS models; see Appendix 5.2.

7. This is not simply an aggregation effect. Mean involvement levels do not gradually increase as the percent minority in a school increases, and for the formal participation model, there are no residual within-school race/ethnic differences. It is only when minority concentration goes above 41% for African Americans and 51% for Hispanics, that the parents' participation levels significantly increase.

8. Although these schools are largely disadvantaged, it should be noted that they are not exclusively inner-city schools. Such schools are included in this group but schools from working class communities and from noncentral city locations are also contained in the sample. The salient commonality is their predominant minority constituency.

9. The estimated effects for the other variables were insignificant and are, thus, not displayed.

10. The reader will notice that the percent Hispanic teacher variable is not included, in this and following models. The percentage of Hispanic teachers in non-Hispanic schools is extremely small. Consequently, separating the effect of the concentration of Hispanic students from the percentage of Hispanic teachers, with this data, is not possible. The profile of Hispanic teachers in regard to the amount of time they spend contacting parents is similar to their African American

counterparts. We suspect that their presence similarly has a positive influence on parental involvement in Hispanic schools. Nevertheless, given the distribution of the teachers, we are unable to demonstrate the general effect.

11. We should caution about drawing immediate policy recommendations from these results. Qualitative studies of the interaction of parents with teachers in minority and nonminority schools would be essential to understanding the general patterns which we have presented.

12. As might be expected, these teachers in general have less formal education and less experience. Somewhat surprisingly though, these characteristics are associated with higher interaction with parents. Corwin and Wagenaar (1976) demonstrate this association. They attribute it to the increased professionalism of teachers with higher degrees and longer tenure. Those teachers tend to exert more autonomy in their approach to education while incorporating parents less.

13. We do not present one single composite model because interactions between the many variables render some of the estimates uninterpretable.

14. The latter is measured by the principal's report of the accuracy of the following statements for the school: (1) Teachers at this school encourage students to do their best; (2) Teachers take the time to respond to students' individual needs; and (3) Students are expected to do homework.

15. See Chapter 2 for a fuller discussion of educational expectations of minority parents for their children.

16. This observation does not imply that these schools necessarily have strong academic environments. Many correlates of academic achievement at the school level are not considered in this chapter. Our focus has been on parental involvement which is, of course, not the primary objective of schools.

Appendix 5.1

A two-stage process was utilized in selecting parents and schools that were included in the analysis. First, individual-level cases were considered. Because of the extremely small sample size, Native American respondents were removed. In addition, cases for which there were no data from parents were excluded. Second, schools were excluded which had fewer than ten cases in the sample. This was necessary in order to have reliable school-level parameter estimates. This subsample contained 22,150 parents and their students and 955 schools. Comparison with the full sample did not reveal any systematic bias. The racial composition as well as socioeconomic status of the sample remained the same. Schools were slightly more urban.

Each model was weighted utilizing the sample weights provided in the NELS:88 dataset. (See the *Base Year: Student Component Data File User's Manual* for a description of the weighting.) These weights were normed to adjust for the mean design effect. Because of the stratified sampling technique in NELS:88, the individual-level weights contain both a component for the probability of the school being selected and a component for the probability of a student being selected within a school. In the HLM, these components were separated to correspond to the levels of analysis in the models.

The following is a list for variables employed in the analysis. (The source variable labels from NELS:88 are given in parentheses.) Correlation matrices of independent variables with the outcome variables are presented as well as correlations of the independent variables with themselves. Means and standard deviations are also included.

Dependent Variables

1. CONTACT: frequency of parent-initiated contact with the school about the child's academic performance (byp58a) and academic program (byp58b).

2. FORMAL: involvement in the parent-teacher organization as measured by the sum of three responses. Do you or your spouse (1) belong to a PTO (byp59a); (2) attend meetings of a PTO (byp59b); and (3) take part in the activities of a PTO (byp59c)?

Individual-Level Variables

1. SES: a composite variable, averaging the nonmissing values of five standardized components (father's and mother's educational levels, father's and mother's occupations, and family income) (byses).

2. GRADES: an average, with all nonmissing elements equally weighted, of student self-reports for grades over four subject areas (bygrads).

3. PAREXP: report of what level of education parent expects child to achieve (0 - less than high school; 1 - high school or GED; 2 - some college; 3 - college degree; 4 - graduate or professional degree) (byp76).

4. BLACK: a dummy variable for African Americans (1 - African American; 0 - otherwise) (race).

5. HISPAN: a dummy variable for Hispanics (1 - Hispanic; 0 - otherwise) (race).

6. ASIAN: a dummy variable for Asians (1 - Asian; 0 - otherwise) (race).

7. SEX: a dummy variable for gender of child (1 - female; 0 - male) (sex).

8. NOSIBS: number of siblings the student has (byp3a).

9. INVOL1: measure of directed discussion of current academic program with parents (bys36a), discussion of high school program with mother (bys50a), and discussion of high program with father (bys50b). These variables are scaled from 0 to 2 and are summed to construct the variable.

10. INVOL2: measure of general talking about current school experiences. The variable is a sum of frequency of discussion of school activities with parents (by36b) and frequency of discussion of things studies in class (bys36c).

11. TWOFT: a dummy variable for two biological parent family with both parents working (byfcomp, byp32, byp33a, byp35, byp36a).

12. TWOPT: a dummy variable for two biological parent family with neither parent working full-time (byfcomp, byp32, byp33a, byp35, byp36a).

13. SINGFT: a dummy variable for single-head household with parent working full-time (byfcomp, byp32, byp33a, byp35, byp36a).

14. SINGPT: a dummy variable for single-head household with parent not working full-time (byfcomp, byp32, byp33a, byp35, byp36a).

15. STEP1FT: a dummy variable for step parent family with 1 parent working full-time (byfcomp, byp32, byp33a, byp35, byp36a).

16. STEP2FT: a dummy variable for step parent family with both parents working full-time (byfcomp, byp32, byp33a, byp35, byp36a).

17. STEPPT: a dummy variable for step parent family with neither parent working full-time (byfcomp, byp32, byp33a, byp35, byp36a).

18. BLK.GRAD: an interaction variable for African American grades (BLACK x GRADES).

School-Level Variables

1. AVSES: average social class background for the school (byses).

2. PBLK: a dummy variable for largely African American schools (1 - over 41% African American; 0 - otherwise) (bysc13d).

3. PHISP: a dummy variable for largely Hispanic schools (1 - over 51% Hispanic; 0 - otherwise) (bysc13c).

4. PCONT: proportion of parents contacted three or more time about the student's academic program and high school placement (byp57b, byp57c, byp57d).

5. PBLKTCH: proportion of African American teachers in the school (bysc20d).

6. PHISPTCH: proportion of Hispanic teachers in the school (bysc20c).

7. TCHTIME: average hours per week teachers spend contacting parents (byt3_30h).

8. TCHINFO: proportion of parents who receive information frequently from teachers (hes26c).

9. PARHS: a dummy variable indicating if parents visit the prospective high school (hes21g).

10. PDISHS: percent of students who talk to teacher or guidance counselor about high school program (bys51aa, bys51ab).

11. HSTEST: a dummy variable indicating if standardized tests are use in assigning students to high school course and programs (bysc35).

12. DISACA: how regularly academic problems and improvement strategies are discussed with the students (hes8f, hes8g).

13. HWPOL: a dummy variable indicating if school has a policy on frequency of homework assignments (hes23j2).

14. PRESS: presence of academic emphasis in the school. The variable is an average of the principles report on a scale of 1 to 5 on the following items: teachers at this school encourage students to do their best (bysc47e); teachers take the time to respond to students' individual needs (bysc47m); and students are expected to do homework (bysc47f).

Table 5.A.1 Individual-level correlations with dependent variables

		Contact	Formal
1	SES	.173**	.289**
2	GRADES	-.103**	.170**
3	PAREXP	.045**	.214**
4	BLACK	.006	.016*
5	HISPAN	.003	-.047**
6	ASIAN	-.032**	-.004
7	SEX	-.117**	-.010
8	NOSIBS	-.032**	.074**
9	INVOL	1.054**	.130**
10	INVOL	2.032**	.117**
11	TWOFT	.025**	.057**
12	TWOPT	-.031**	-.044**
13	SINGFT	-.010	-.063**
14	SINGPT	-.024**	-.064**
15	STEP1FT	-.001	-.049**
16	STEP2FT	.024**	-.038**
17	STEPPT	-.024**	-.044**
18	BLK.GRAD	-.001	.067**
	Mean	1.090	.895
	SD	1.185	1.096

Table 5.A.2 School-level correlations with dependent variables

		Average contact	Average formal
1	AVSES	.344**	.554**
2	PBLK	.017	-.040
3	PHISP	-.006	-.051
4	PCONT	.406**	.212**
5	PBLKTCH	.026	-.063
6	PHISPTCH	.003	.018
7	TCHTIME	.115**	.145**
8	TCHINFO	.043	.141**
9	PARHS	.186**	.256**
10	PDISHS	.095**	.077*
11	HSTEST	.111**	.137**
12	DISACA	-.040	.043
13	HWPOL	.097**	.261**
14	PRESS	.155**	.322**
	Mean	1.146	1.096
	SD	.379	.641

* = significant at .05 level; ** = significant at .01 level (2-tailed)

† These variables are not adjusted for the individual-level characteristics of parents as in the HLM models (see Appendix 5.2)

Table 5.A.3 Individual-level variables: correlation coefficients

	1	2	3	4	5	6	7	8	9	10	11	12	13	14	15	16	17	18
1 SES																		
2 GRADES	.323**																	
3 PAREXP	.426**	.405**																
4 BLACK	-.211**	-.092**	-.006															
5 HISPAN	-.196**	-.067**	-.028**	-.127**														
6 ASIAN	.052**	.069**	.084**	-.072**	-.060**													
7 SEX	-.026**	.103*	.045**	.007	-.000	-.007												
8 NOSIBS	-.214**	-.107*	-.113**	.099**	.105**	-.010	.021**											
9 INVOL1	.217**	.276**	.225**	-.041**	-.027**	-.000	.067**	-.100**										
10 INVOL2	.231**	.281**	.227**	-.047**	-.070**	-.027**	.103**	-.072**	.460**									
11 TWOFT	.158**	.065**	.070**	-.052**	-.027**	.055**	-.020**	-.152**	.060**	.025**								
12 TWOPT	-.142**	-.034**	-.061**	.001	.079**	.033**	.005	.083**	-.017	-.033**	-.153**							
13 SINGFT	-.065**	-.068**	-.007	.127**	-.018**	-.029**	.003	-.053**	-.083**	-.036**	-.226**	-.088**						
14 SINGPT	-.259**	-.102**	-.062**	.190**	.021**	-.026**	.013	.056**	-.0859**	-.048**	-.158**	-.062**	-.091**					
15 STEP1FT	-.050**	-.046*	-.041**	-.007	-.006	-.017	.016*	.127**	-.030**	-.020**	-.157**	-.062**	-.091**	-.064**				
16 STEP2FT	.021*	-.039*	-.029**	.014*	-.008	-.022**	.012	.106**	-.023**	-.002	-.175**	-.069**	-.101**	-.071**	-.071**			
17 STEPPT	-.103**	-.047**	-.042**	.034**	.001	-.009	.004	.073**	-.048**	-.019**	-.089**	-.035**	-.052**	-.036**	-.036**	-.040**		
18 BLK.GRAD	.133**	.344**	.094**	-.251**	.032**	.018**	.042**	-.056**	.074**	.062**	.036**	-.005	-.025**	-.118**	-.001	.017*	-.038**	
Mean	-.109	2.896	2.432	.132	.096	.033	.499	2.262	3.747	2.898	.281	.056	.115	.060	.059	.073	.020	.351
SD	.752	.755	1.267	.338	.295	.178	.500	1.560	1.648	1.090	.449	.231	.319	.238	.237	.260	.140	.942

* = significant at .05 level; ** = significant at .01 level (2-tailed)

Table 5.A.4 School-level variables: correlation coefficients

	1	2	3	4	5	6	7	8	9	10	11	12	13	14
1 AVSES														
2 PBLK	-.060													
3 PHISP	-.051	.290**												
4 PCONT	.165**	-.015	.127**											
5 PBLKTCH	-.317**	.213**	.018	.028										
6 PHISPTCH	-.067	.009	.068	.129**	.032									
7 TCHTIME	-.011	.047	.166**	.100**	.090*	.014								
8 TCHINFO	.089*	.046	.063	.079*	-.004	.068	.006							
9 PARHS	.225**	.061	.086*	.122**	.010	-.031	.113**	.093*						
10 PDISHS	-.073*	.148**	.116**	.300**	.201**	.089*	-.004	-.012	.120**					
11 HSTEST	.049	.144**	.123**	.077*	.061	-.001	.071*	.044	.238**	.159**				
12 DISACA	-.135**	.028	.019	.099*	.156**	.113**	.138**	.185**	.061	-.004	.160**			
13 HWPOL	.132**	.092*	.056	.107*	.151**	-.026	.041	.126**	.286**	.067	.182**	.067		
14 PRESS	.263**	-.004	-.006	.068	-.090*	-.012	.073*	.183**	.205**	-.016	.129**	.106*	.083*	
Mean	-.088	.084	.040	.038	.069	.023	.858	.401	.482	.570	.559	5.643	.624	4.256
SD	.462	.278	.197	.037	.163	.100	.579	.293	.500	.224	.497	2.413	.485	.617

* = significant at .05 level; ** = significant at .01 level (2-tailed)

Appendix 5.2

This paper considers effects on parental involvement at two levels of analysis: (1) the effects of parent and student characteristics on involvement within schools, and (2) the characteristics of the school that affect mean levels of participation. HLM fits models that correspond to each level. At the parent level, involvement is predicted within each school:

$$(involvement)_{0j} = \beta_{00} + \beta_{1j}(SES)_{ij} + \beta_{2j}(Hispanic)_{ij} + \beta_{3j}(African\ American)_{ij} + \beta_{5j}(grades)_{ij} + r_{ij} \tag{1}$$

The β coefficients (which can be allowed to vary across schools) serve as dependent variables in the school-level equation(s):

$$\beta_{0j} = \pi_{00} + \pi_{01}(average\ SES)_j + \pi_{02}(\%African\ American)j + \tau_{0j} \tag{2}$$

In the school level equations, β_{0j} represents the schools' mean participation rate adjusted for the individual-level characteristics of parents included in equation 1. In HLM, these equations are estimated simultaneously, using the EM algorithm to obtain maximum likelihood estimates of the variance components, which are then used to generate the β and π coefficients.

Traditional contextual analysis estimates the entire model at the individual level, assigning the values of school-level variables to parents and students within schools. The following contextual equation is equivalent to the two-level HLM presented above:

$$(involvement)_i = \beta_0 + \beta_1(SES)_i + \beta_2(Hispanic)_i + \beta_3(African\ American)_i + \beta_5(grades)_i + \beta_6(average\ SES)_i + \beta_7(\%\ African\ American)_i + \varepsilon_i \tag{3}$$

The relationship between the individual-level effect for African American parents in the OLS contextual analysis compared to the HLM is not straightforward. Let us call the individual-level effect (which occurs within school) B_w and the effect at the school level (between schools) B_b. The OLS estimate of β_3 when % African American in the school is not in the equation is a combination of B_w and B_b. In most cases, this blend of effects is not interpretable. The influence of B_b on B_w can be controlled as in the contextual analysis but the estimate of the individual-level effect continues to include the influence of other school-level characteristics that may not be included in the model. That is, school-level characteristic that are correlated with the individual-level African American variable and with the dependent variable, but are not included in the model, will bias the estimation of β_3. The HLM estimate of β_{3j} in each school is strictly an estimate of B_w.

In addition, even if these other concerns can be adequately addressed, the OLS estimation of β_3 continues to be inadequate because the standard errors for these coefficients are negatively biased. By estimating equations at two levels, HLM partitions error variance into its within-school and between-school components (r_{ij}, τ_j). Contextual analysis fails to represent explicitly the random variation in its two parts. Because the level 1 observations are clustered into the level 2 groups (i.e., parents within particular schools), the assumption of independent errors in the individual-level model (Equation 3) is violated. This violation leads to underestimated standard errors and thus an overestimation of significance (see Goldberger and Cain (1982) for a discussion of this issue using the High School and Beyond dataset). In contrast, by estimating distinct school and individual level errors, HLM adjusts for the correlation of errors within schools (Bryk and Raudenbush 1992).

The contextual analysis estimates for the individual-level race effects in the two-parental involvement variables are as follows:

Contextual analysis estimates of race effects

Dependent variable	Estimated coefficient	
	African American	Hispanic
Academic contact	.169***	.126***
PTO participation	.256***	.013

*** = significant at .001 level

These estimates are in-between the strictly individual-level OLS estimates and the within school HLM estimates, though they are much closer to the individual-level model. (See Table 5.1 and 5.3 for comparison.) The contextual estimates are, in general, twice that of the HLM analysis. This suggests that other factors at the school-level are influencing the contextual analysis coefficients. However, it is important to note that we would not be able to make this statement without an accurate estimate of B_w, and this estimate comes from the HLM analysis. HLM analytically separates the within and between school effects. Thus, we have an unbiased estimate of B_w that is not blended with the effects of B_b or any other school-level characteristics.

6

Parent Choice and Inequality

James S. Coleman, Kathryn S. Schiller, and Barbara Schneider

One form of parental involvement in a child's education is choice of a school. Many parents exercise choice of their children's schools as part of deciding where to live—in what part of the city, in which suburb, in which neighborhood. A few exercise choice of a school by sending their children to private schools rather than local public schools. For other parents, choice among public schools without change of residence is possible, either through the existence of a few magnet schools in the district or through a system of choice throughout the district, such as open enrollment or easy transfers between schools.

Despite these choices that some parents make, most parents experience severe constraints on this form of involvement in their children's education. For parents in sparsely populated areas, there is only one school within reasonable distance of their residence. These parents have no choice simply due to geographic constraints. Other parents have no choice because they lack the resources to live in a desirable residential area. In choosing school and residence, preferences among schools must be balanced against the cost of living in a particular school attendance zone. For example, in the Hyde Park neighborhood in Chicago, town houses on the north side of 55th Street sell for about 25% less than identical town houses on the south side of the same street. This street is the boundary between school attendance zones; the school south of 55th Street is racially mixed and attended largely by middle class families, many of them children of University of Chicago faculty. The school north of 55th Street is nearly all black and has many children from families with considerably lower incomes and educational levels. Constraints on the exercise of choice of a school are especially strong for those families that are geographically isolated, have a low income, or are subject to residential discrimination due to race or ethnicity. Constraints are least strong for those of high income in metropolitan areas which have numerous suburbs and a supply of private schools.

The level of this form of parental involvement as it is manifested in choice of private schools is very low, as a direct consequence of the fact that public schooling is free, while private schooling is costly. Private school enroll-ments represent a small percentage of the total elementary and secondary school population. For example, the percentage of eighth graders in private schools in the United States in 1988, as estimated by the NELS:88 data, is 9.5%, which is 360,000 students out of a total of 3 million. This number consists of about 315,000 children in religiously-affiliated schools, and about 45,000 children in other private schools.

The high cost of private schools can be shown by estimating the financial sacrifice a family of average income makes to send its children to a private school. Using the per pupil expenditure on education in American public schools as a measure ($4,227 in 1988,[1] averaged over the country for both elementary and secondary schools), the cost of schooling for two children is 27% of the median family income.[2] Many private schools (principally those with a religious sponsorship) are lower in cost than this, and some private schools (generally, the "independent" schools) are higher in cost. Nevertheless, this figure of $4,227 compared to median family income gives some indication of the financial sacrifice that would be necessary for a moderate income family to make the choice of a private school. For a family of median income with two children, a sacrifice of 27% of total income is hardly possible, because it would ordinarily exceed the family's discretionary income.

It is not surprising that this form of parental involvement in a child's education is minimal in the United States. In many foreign countries, private schools are financed wholly or largely by public funds, and, in some Western European countries, they enroll a much larger fraction of the total population of children than in the United States.

The Policy Issue of Parental Choice

In recent years, parental choice of a school, in contrast to school district assignment of children to a school (most often on the basis of residence in a public school's "attendance zone"), has emerged as a major policy issue in education. The debate has two forms, corresponding to two ranges of choice. The first form is assignment of children to a particular public school by the school district versus parental choice among public schools in the district (or, in some cases, public schools in other districts). The second form of the debate is the extension of choice beyond the public sector, to include private schools, without cost (or with little cost) to parents.

This second form includes the question of whether public funds should be used to support enrollment in private schools, and, if so, what form should such aid take. The two forms of support most extensively discussed are tuition tax credits (in which parents whose children attend private schools would receive credits on their state or federal income taxes for some part of the tuition cost of their children's schooling) or a tuition voucher (in which the parent would be given a "voucher" which can be used at any approved school). Vouchers are ordinarily seen to encompass choice among public schools as well as choice outside the public sector, but tuition tax credits have no implications for choice among schools in the public sector.

Within the past few years, there has been a considerable expansion of school choice within the public sector, allowing parents to choose a school other than the one to which their child would be assigned based on residence. One clear example of this is magnet school programs, most frequently found at the high school level in larger cities (often introduced to facilitate stable school desegregation), sometimes with racial quotas, sometimes without them. In addition to magnet programs, some school districts, such as District 4 in New York City, and Cambridge, Massachusetts, have adopted open choice programs in which parents can elect to send their child to any school in the district. In most cases, such choice is without a guarantee of receiving one's first choice, because of space limitations and in some cases racial quotas. There is one statewide policy (Minnesota), in which parents can choose to send their child to a particular school in another school district, but may not (depending upon district policy) be able to choose among schools within the district in which they reside.[3]

The Issue of Inequality

A major question regarding school choice concerns the effect expanded choice will have on inequality of educational opportunity. This is not, of course, the only question about the consequences of choice. Quite apart from the effect on inequality is the overall effect on educational outcomes: Would choice generally improve those outcomes or degrade them? In addition, the question of satisfaction of children and parents with school is important. There are also questions about the effects of private school choice on racial, religious, or economic divisiveness in society. Nevertheless, a major question is that of the distributional effects: Would extensive expansion of choice provide more benefits for the educationally advantaged or for the educationally disadvantaged? Would expansion of choice increase educational inequality or decrease it?

The NELS:88 data can provide some insights into the question of who would make more use of school choice if it were expanded. In these analyses, we will compare the predicted response to choice for African Americans, Hispanics, Asian Americans, and non-Hispanic whites. In addition, we will compare the predicted response for parents of three educational levels (based on the highest education of either parent): high school only; some education beyond high school; and a 4-year college degree or more.

There are grounds for believing that expansion of choice would increase inequality of educational opportunity, and grounds for believing that it would reduce inequality. On the former side is the argument that by giving parents greater opportunity for school choice, those parents with greater economic resources and educational knowledge would be more likely to take advantage of school choice, and their children would gain the most. Disadvantaged racial and ethnic minorities and poorly-educated parents would be even more disadvantaged than at present, unable to benefit from the opportunity provided by choice.

On the other side is the argument that because school assignment is currently determined by residence (except for those with sufficient money to opt out of the public system by paying tuition for a private school), this creates effective constraints only for the poor, because it is they who cannot choose place of residence. They, according to this argument, would gain most by having more options, because they now have the least, being unable to afford private schools where they live. This argument contends that disadvantaged parents are not indifferent about choice and would become knowledgeable choosers, because they have the most to gain by being able to choose "good" schools.

These opposing arguments can, in principle, be settled by empirical evidence. Research in school districts which have expanded choice could show the rates with which different groups of parents (for example, parents differing on such factors as race/ethnicity, family income, parental educational levels) choose a school other than the one to which their children are assigned. Some districts in the United States have programs for which such analyses could be conducted at the eighth grade, but school choice is most frequent in magnet school programs at the high school level. Even there, problems for an analysis of who takes advantage of choice opportunities are not trivial. In Minneapolis, which has a program of relatively free choice, desegregation rules place different constraints on the movement of African American and white children, thus defeating a racial comparison of response to choice.

The NELS:88 data provide indirect evidence relevant to these arguments, and thus relevant to the question of the potential effect of expansion of opportunity for parental choice on inequality of educational opportunity. The question can be separated into two parts: one concerning choice among public schools and the other concerning choice of a private school. In both, we can ask the following question: What would be the response of parents of children from different backgrounds if their opportunities for choice were the same? We will examine the question of choice among public schools first.

Public School Choice

In elementary schools, there is little choice among public schools, other than through choice of residence. The choice that does exist was not assessed well in the NELS:88 data collection. Thus, to obtain some indication of how students and parents from various backgrounds might respond to increased opportunities for choice, it is necessary to look beyond eighth grade.

Students were asked what high school they were most likely to attend. They were also asked if they were considering another high school, and, if they were considering another, they were asked to give the name of that school and indicate whether it was public or private. From these questions, it is possible to classify students into the following categories: (1) those considering only one public high school, (2) those considering only one private high school, (3) those considering two public high schools, (4) those considering one public high school and one private high school, (5) those considering two private high schools.

Only those students in the third category can be regarded as exercising choice among public schools, while students in the first category are regarded as not exercising public school choice. Those exercising private school choice are excluded from this part of the analysis. We may ask how likely students from different backgrounds are to exercise choice among public high schools rather than to limit themselves to a single public high school. This can give some indication of the degree to which students and parents from different backgrounds are likely to respond to an expansion of choice among public schools.

There is, however, one major difficulty in using these data to answer this question. This is the fact that current opportunities for choice among public high schools differ greatly for different students, and differ in ways that may be systematic across different social backgrounds. For example, public school choice for eighth grade students is most extensive in some large central cities which have a number of high schools, including in some cases magnet schools, specialized high schools, or both. Choice among public high schools is less extensive in suburban and rural school districts, being least so in those school districts with a single public high school.

Because racial and ethnic groups are differently distributed across central city, suburban, small town, and rural school districts, a misleading picture of the potential responsiveness to choice is obtained by examining the current likelihood of considering more than one high school. In particular, white students are more likely to reside in school districts with a single high school, and thus be currently constrained to limiting their consideration of high schools to a single school. For example, in the NELS:88 sample, there are 12,700 white students in the first or third categories, and, of them, 15.2% were in the third category—that is, they were considering more than one public school. There are 4,054 African American, Hispanic, or Asian students in these two categories, and, of them, 31.1% were considering more than one school. Without taking into account the constraints on choice due to the limited number of high schools in the district—constraints that would be removed by full choice across districts—one would immediately conclude that whites would be much less likely to exercise choice than would students from other ethnic and racial groups. That conclusion, however, cannot be drawn without taking into account current opportunities for choice.

We would like to assess what the tendency to exercise choice is for various minority groups and for students from differing parental education backgrounds, freed from the varying opportunities for choice of high school due to availability and district policy. To make this assessment, the first task is to find the opportunity for choice of high school, for each of the groups under consideration, given the schools they attend.

The way this is done is described in Appendix 6.1. The general idea is this: First, the opportunity for choice in each public eighth grade school is estimated using the proportion of students in the school who are considering more than one public school (based on the number who mentioned only public schools, the first and third categories in the above list). But this proportion must be standardized for the characteristics of the students in that school—that is, they should be freed from the special tendencies toward or away from exercising choice due to the particular characteristics of students in that school. (This estimate of the opportunity in a school will differ slightly for different students, because for each individual student the estimate is based on the *other* students in the same school, excluding that student's own actions. This estimate for student h in school j is labelled d_{hj} in Appendix 6.1.) Then the opportunity for choice for each group under consideration is calculated by finding the average opportunity for that

TABLE 6.1 Opportunities for choice for various groups, expressed as the average proportion considering more than one public high school in schools attended by each group, if the schools' student bodies were standardized to the sample as a whole

	Average opportunity
All students	.191
(SD)	(.137)
Race/Ethnicity	
African Americans	.239
Asian Americans	.250
Hispanics	.217
Whites	.178
Parents' education	
High school or less	.190
Some college	.197
College graduate	.181

group, which is the average over schools, weighted by the number of students from that group in the school. (This is labelled d_k for group k in Appendix 6.1.)

These levels of opportunity for each of the subgroups under consideration are shown in Table 6.1. This table presents the proportion of students in the schools attended by each group who would be expected to consider more than one school, standardized for the student bodies in those schools. It shows that, as expected, opportunity in the schools attended by whites is lower than that of any other racial/ethnic group. The opportunity for African and Asian Americans is highest, probably because they are concentrated in central cities. Hispanics are near the level of Asian and African Americans, but slightly lower. The groups with differing parental educational levels are much more alike in the levels of opportunity for choice in their schools.

These proportions, of course, do not represent the overall levels of opportunity for choice among public high schools for these groups, because choice of school is partly exercised through a residential choice made earlier. That form of opportunity varies greatly for different groups due to income levels and to residential discrimination affecting some of them. Among the groups examined here, whites and those with high educational levels have the greatest opportunity of residential choice. The exercise of such choice, by moving to suburbs with smaller school districts with fewer schools, tends to reduce the opportunity for choice exhibited in Table 6.1. This is because it often involves moving from a district with a number of high schools to a district with only one.

We may use the estimate of opportunity for choice as shown in Table 6.1 to find the opportunity-standardized *exercise* of choice by each of these

TABLE 6.2[4] Actual choice, expected choice, actual minus expected, and opportunity-standardized choice for racial/ethnic and parents' education groups

	(1) Actual choice	(2) Expected choice	(3)= (1)-(2) Actual expected	(4) = (3)+.191 Opportunity-standardized
Race/Ethnicity				
African American	.359	.239	+.120	.311
Asian American	.269	.250	+.019	.210
Hispanic	.246	.217	+.029	.220
White	.153	.178	-.025	.166
Parents' education				
High school or less	.197	.190	+.007	.198
Some college	.210	.197	+.013	.204
College graduate	.147	.181	-.034	.157

groups. Table 6.2 gives the proportion of students from different social backgrounds who are considering more than one public high school relative to the opportunity in their 8th grade school. The technique is described in detail in Appendix 6.1, but briefly it is calculated as follows: The difference between the actual choice and estimated opportunity for each group is added to the proportion exercising choice overall. The actual proportion of students from a given background that are considering more than one school (which is our measure of exercise of choice) is directly calculable from the data (as the quantity c_k in Appendix 6.1) and is shown in Column 1. The estimate of opportunity taken from Table 6.1 and shown in Column 2 can be interpreted as the expected proportion exercising choice. The difference between the actual and the expected is the excess or deficiency in the proportion considering more than one school for the given group—or Column 1 minus Column 2, shown in Column 3. Finally, in Column 4, the overall mean is added back in to give the expected proportion of students from the group in question considering more than one school, standardized for the opportunity provided by the schools they attend. Thus, Column 4 is an opportunity-standardized measure of the exercise of choice by each of the groups shown in the table.

Perhaps the most striking results in this table are those concerning whites and parents with college degrees. They exercise low levels of choice, both actual and opportunity-standardized. The level of actual choice is in both cases below the expected choice, that is, the student-body-standardized level of choice exercised in the schools they attend. When adjusted for opportunity in the schools they attend, as shown in Column 4, they are still considerably below the other groups shown in the table. At the other extreme are African American students. The actual proportion considering more than one high school is very high, with 35.9% mentioning more than one public high school, and the opportunity-standardized level of choice remains high, at 31.1% mentioning more than one high school. After opportunity is standardized, the especially low proportions of whites and students from high educational backgrounds considering more than one high school and the especially high proportions of African American students doing so indicate that opportunity is not the sole source of differences among racial/ethnic groups and educational background groups.

There are two other likely sources of these differences. One is that many students do not consider more than a single school, because choices have been made earlier with parents' choice of residence. This is most likely to be true for whites and for students from high educational backgrounds; it is least likely to be true for African American students. Another source of difference is that some students are uncertain about their living situations. Thus, instability of one's family situation, which is most frequent for African Americans and students from low educational backgrounds, may lead to mentioning more than one high school.

The effect of this second factor can be directly assessed, by standardizing groups according to background characteristics that might affect family instability. Those family characteristics that showed some effect on considering more than one school are having a single parent family, living with a stepparent, some other family arrangement other than living with natural parents, parents' education, parents' expectation for child's education, and family income. (See Appendix 6.2 for descriptions of these variables.) When the group that is most extreme in considering more than one school, African Americans, is adjusted to the population means on these variables, the percent considering more than one school is reduced only to 32.5% from 35.9%. That is, African American students who are like the national average in family background are only slightly less likely to consider more than one high school than is the average African American student. When both family background and opportunity are standardized to the national average, the percentage considering more than one school is still 27.7%, that is higher than the actual or opportunity-standardized choice for any of the other groups. This indicates that the variations in family background and opportunity account for only a part of the differences among groups in proportions considering more than a single high school, and that neither greater opportunity for choice nor greater instability of background accounts for the major part of the greater likelihood of considering more than one high school. The major portion appears to be due to differences among racial and ethnic groups in the exercise of choice, given comparable family situations and comparable opportunities for choice.

In the exercise of choice by students classified by parents' education, there is an indication in Table 6.2 that choice is greatest, not among those with the lowest educational background, but among those with a somewhat higher educational background. This suggests that the arguments for expanding opportunity for choice would increase inequality of opportunity might not be altogether wrong: it may be that the least well educated families are less likely to take advantage of opportunities for choice. This result makes the frequent exercise of choice by minority students especially impressive.

On average, African American and Hispanic students have parents with considerably lower educational backgrounds than do whites. The lower exercise of choice among students with less-well-educated parents would lead one to anticipate lower rates of choice among these two groups rather than higher choice, as compared to whites. What, then, is the case for lower educated minorities? Do they show the low-educated pattern (less exercise of choice than the middle educational group) or the minority pattern (high exercise of choice relative to whites)?

We examine the exercise of choice by the African American, Hispanic, and white students of each educational group to address this question.[5] Table 6.3 shows the actual choice and opportunity-standardized choice (comparable to Columns 1 and 4 from Table 6.2) for the three educational

TABLE 6.3 Actual choice and opportunity-standardized choice for three educational levels within racial/ethnic groups

		(1)	(2)
		Actual choice	Opportunity-standardized choice
African American			
	High school or less	.330	.306
	Some college	.389	.324
	College graduate	.335	.287
Hispanic			
	High school or less	.248	.218
	Some college	.249	.227
	College graduate	.224	.201
White			
	High school or less	.150	.165
	Some college	.170	.178
	College graduate	.126	.145

levels within each of the three racial/ethnic groups. This table shows that the pattern among parental education groups is the same for all three racial and ethnic groups, and the pattern among racial and ethnic groups is the same for all three parents' education groups. Specifically, the middle education group is highest; and among racial and ethnic groups, African Americans are highest, Hispanics second, and whites third.

It is true, then, as the right-hand column of Table 6.3 shows, that children with the lowest-educated parents do not exercise choice as often as do those whose parents have some college education. But even the minorities with least well-educated parents—high school or less—are considerably more likely to exercise choice than are any of the white parent-education groups.

What About Expansion of Choice?

While minorities seem more likely to exercise choice, we are as yet unable to say anything about their responsiveness to expansion of opportunity to choose. We can gain some idea of what this responsiveness would be by projecting what the frequency of choice would be in the group if the opportunity for choice were greatly increased.[6] This is done by regressing the exercise of choice (i.e., considering more than one high school) on both background characteristics and the opportunity for choice in a school (d_{hj} in Appendix 6.1). This gives a measure, for each group, of the expected increase in choice as the opportunity for choice is increased. Multiplying the exponential of the logistic regression coefficients for opportunity by the increased opportunity for choice if choice were unrestricted gives the increase in an individual's likelihood of exercising choice if choice were unrestricted. The proportion exercising choice (by considering more than one high school) if choice were "unrestricted" is taken to be the existing proportion for all students (.191) taken from Table 6.1 plus two standard deviations (.191 + .274 = .465). The difference between this "unrestricted" choice and the opportunity for choice that currently exists for a given group is the measure of the increased opportunity for choice for that group. The calculation of predicted levels of choice for each group resulting from expansion of choice is given by equation (11) in Appendix 6.1. Column 1 in Table 6.4 shows the actual proportion considering more than one school, taken from Table 6.2. In Column 2 is shown the predicted proportion considering more than one high school if the opportunity in their schools were raised to the level at which 46.5% considered more than one high school, illustrating the effect of increased opportunity.

Table 6.4 shows considerable differences among racial and ethnic groups in their exercise of choice as opportunity increases. The predicted effects of existing levels of exercise of choice augmented by the specified

TABLE 6.4 Predicted proportions exercising choice if choice were expanded for racial/ethnic and parents' education groups[7]

	(1)	(2)
	Actual choice	Predicted proportion exercising choice
Race/Ethnicity		
African American	.359	.558
Asian American	.269	.373
Hispanic	.246	.380
White	.153	.349
Parents' education		
High school or less	.197	.363
Some college	.210	.387
College graduate	.147	.367

increase in opportunity to .465, shown in Column 2, indicate that African Americans would exercise choice far more than any other group, with over 50% considering more than one high school. Hispanics and Asian Americans are next, and whites are lowest. The high predicted proportion for African Americans is especially noteworthy because their existing level of opportunity is higher than that of any other group except Asian Americans (see Table 6.1). It is their high responsiveness to the level of opportunity that makes their predicted proportion due to increased opportunity so high. Students differing in parents' education are very close in predicted levels of choice; the somewhat greater responsiveness of college background families to expansion of opportunity partially makes up for their lower current levels of choice.

There are, of course, many caveats to these projections, as well as to the analysis as a whole. First, the projections assume that a policy of open choice in public schools would bring the same level of opportunity for choice to all groups. However, low population density in small towns and rural areas creates a natural limitation on choice that would not be overcome by policy changes. This would limit opportunity most for whites, who are disproportionately located in areas of low population density, and would likely make the differences between the minority groups and whites in exercise of choice greater than that shown in Column 2. This is indicated by the existing exercise of choice by white students in urban, suburban, and rural areas. The overall proportion of whites considering more than one high school is .152, as shown in Table 6.2. But for eighth graders in rural areas, this drops to .132; for those in suburban areas, it is .143; for those in cities it rises to .249. The low level of exercise of choice in rural areas compared to those in urban areas is largely due to low population density, which would not be overcome by a change in policy.

A second caveat is one that exists for all inferences about effects based on statistical analysis of non-experimental data. The greater predicted responsiveness of African Americans to expanded opportunity could be due to differences between the high-opportunity schools and the low-opportunity schools on variables that are not measured in characterizing the schools according to their opportunity for choice. However, there is consistency between the existing levels of opportunity-standardized choice (Column 4 in Table 6.2) and the predicted responsiveness to increase in choice. African Americans are not only located in schools with higher opportunities for choice but also more likely to take advantage of those opportunities than other groups, thus we would expect them to be more responsive if those opportunities were expanded. The rank order of the racial and ethnic groups is the same and that of education groups nearly the same on these two indicators of exercise of choice.

Finally, one must make a caveat concerning the action under study. It is the act of considering more than one public high school. This is something less than exercise of choice. In fact, exercise of choice among public schools is not easily measured without very detailed information. With such information, it would be necessary to characterize both the rigidity of assignment to a high school and the family's response to the degree of freedom that exists.[8]

These caveats should make one cautious about inferences from the analysis, but should not lead to rejection of the inferences. Like all inferences from observations, they can be strengthened or weakened by other data relevant to the inferences. Further analysis later in the paper will examine additional data.

Effects of Choice on Inequality: The First Results

At the outset, we indicated that there were grounds for believing that expansion of choice would increase inequality of educational opportunity as well as grounds for believing that expansion would have the opposite effect, decreasing inequality. The grounds for the first belief were that minority parents would be less likely to take advantage of the increased opportunities. The grounds for the second belief were that the minority parents had much more reason to take advantage of the increased opportunities, because they have been less able to exercise choice through choice of residence.

Nearly all the evidence points to the second effect rather than the first: Minorities, especially African Americans, exercise choice of the kind indicated with these data far more than do whites, even when opportunity for choice is the same. In general, minorities concentrated in cities already

Table 6.5 The proportions of students from four family income groups considering more than one public high school

Income	Proportion considering more than one high school
Less than $12,500	.282
$12,500 - 22,500	.217
$22,501 - 42,500	.161
Greater than $42,500	.150

have more public high schools available to make choice possible, as indicated by their higher opportunity for choice than that of whites, shown in Table 6.1. This of course does not mean that whites have less opportunity for choice, because white parents are far more likely to have had the opportunity for choice of schools through their greater opportunity for choice of residence.

This effect of opportunity for residential choice to depress the proportion considering more than one high school can be shown by examining the proportion of students from families of different income levels who are considering more than one high school. Those families with higher income have greater opportunity to satisfy their choice of high school through choice of residence, and are less likely to want to consider more than one high school, given their existing residential choice. This is evident in the proportions considering more than one public high school for parents with differing levels of income, shown in Table 6.5.

The inference that the low level of choice among high schools by whites is a result of earlier choice of school through choice of residence is reinforced by this table, showing that the level of choice among students from higher income families is lower than that among students from lower-income families. This is consistent with Table 6.2, showing that the current levels of choice among students with best-educated parents is lowest.

Projections of the potential effects of expansion of public school choice indicate that the differences in exercise of choice between whites and minorities would continue, and the black-white differences would increase slightly. Thus, to the degree that choice among schools increases educational opportunity, the indication is that expansion of choice would decrease rather than increase inequality of educational opportunity for African Americans. The evidence for the other minorities is less decisive; but, in general, it indicates that those with most constraints on their residence, currently are most responsive to the opportunities for school choice, and they would continue to be most responsive if opportunities for choice were expanded.

Private School Choice

The constraints on attending private school are quite different from those on public school choice. Many fewer public school students and their parents consider a private high school as a possibility than consider alternative public high schools. While about 20% consider two or more public schools as possibilities, less than 5% mention a private school as a possibility—either as the school they are most likely to attend or as an alternative to the public school they are most likely to attend.

However, geographic location and local school district policy are not the principal constraints for private school choice. Cost of attending a private school is the greatest constraint. For example, among those whose family incomes are below $12,500, only 2.1% mention a private high school as a possibility; for the next income group, up to $42,500, 3.4% mention a private school; and for those with a family income above that, 8.1% mention a private school. As for actual enrollment in private school at 8th grade, only 3.3% of those with incomes below $12,500 are enrolled, compared to 19.5% of those with incomes above $42,500.

As with public school choice, the examination of private school choice involves two questions. The first question concerns what proportion of students from each of the different backgrounds are attending private school in the 8th grade, and what proportion of public school students from each background consider a private high school. The second question concerns what proportion of students from each background would be attending a private school in the 8th grade if money were not a constraint, and what proportion of public school students from each background would consider a private high school if money were not a constraint. This second question cannot be answered well; the only approximation possible with these data is an examination of the number of students attending a private school or mentioning a private high school for students from families with higher income, but other characteristics the same.

The first question is examined in Table 6.6. Column 1 shows the proportion of public school students who are considering attending a private high school. These data show that the proportion of public school eighth grade students considering attendance at a private school is not greatly different for the four racial and ethnic groups. They show, however, that it increases considerably with increase in parents' education. Actual attendance at private schools in the eighth grade shows strikingly different patterns for secular and religious private schools. Column 2 shows that less than one in a hundred 8th graders of African American or Hispanic descent, or parental education less than a college degree attend secular private schools.

TABLE 6.6 The proportion of public school students considering a religiously based or secular private high school, either as the school they are most likely to attend or as an alternative, and the proportion actually attending these schools at the eighth grade level

	Proportion of public school students mentioning private high school	Proportion of all students attending private eighth grade, secular	Proportion of all students attending private eighth grade, religious
All students	.041	.015	.101
Race/Ethnicity			
African American	.033	.005	.052
Asian American	.058	.031	.126
Hispanic	.034	.004	.089
White	.043	.017	.110
Parents' education			
High school or less	.025	.002	.056
Some college	.037	.007	.096
College graduate	.074	.043	.159

It is only the college-graduate parents and the Asian Americans who have more than 2% of their children in secular private schools.

Column 3 shows that the proportions of students in religious private schools (about two-thirds of which are Catholic) ranges from about 5% for African Americans to about 13% for Asian Americans. Comparing these with the proportions of public school students considering a private school in Column 1 shows that the proportion attending religiously-based private schools has about the same gradient with parents' education as those in public schools considering a private high school, about a 3-to-1 ratio for students with a parent having a college degree compared to those with neither parent having more than a high school degree. However, the racial and ethnic comparisons show that the proportion of African American students attending religious schools in the eighth grade is somewhat lower, when compared to the other groups, than the proportion of public school eighth graders considering private high school would suggest. The difference between Hispanics and African Americans, although slight, may be due to the high proportion of Hispanics (.776) who are Catholic, and the low proportion African American (.075), together with the fact that most religiously-based schools are Catholic.

This can be seen in Table 6.7. Column 3 of the table shows that 40.9% of African Americans who are Catholic attend Catholic schools, the highest proportion of any group. Thus, it may be the low proportion of African Americans who are Catholic that keeps their numbers in Catholic schools so low.

TABLE 6.7 Predicted proportion enrolled in religious schools if all were Catholic but remained the same on other background characteristics, for each racial and ethnic group and each parents' education group[9]

	Actual enrollment in religious schools	Proportion Catholic	Proportion of Catholics enrolled in Catholic school	Predicted enrollment if entire group were Catholic
Race/Ethnicity				
African American	.052	.075	.409	.184
Asian American	.126	.334	.176	.255
Hispanic	.089	.776	.101	.098
White	.110	.290	.305	.217
Parents' education				
High school	.056	.303	.164	.116
Some college	.096	.298	.272	.204
College or more	.159	.317	.305	.273

A hypothetical experiment can be carried out, asking what would be the proportions of each group in Catholic schools if all students were Catholic (assuming that Catholic schools were available for the additional students to the same degree as for present Catholics). If these students had the backgrounds of those currently in Catholic schools, that proportion would be given in Column 3: African Americans would show the highest proportions, and Hispanics the lowest. However, if the backgrounds of non-Catholics remained otherwise the same as present, the proportions would be as given by Column 4 of Table 6.7. This column shows the predicted proportions enrolled in religious schools if the whole of each racial or educational group were Catholic, but remained the same on other background characteristics. As Table 6.7 shows, the predicted proportion in religiously-based private schools if all of each group were Catholic (based on the logistic regression equations predicting enrollment with other background characteristics controlled) is not greatly different for African Americans, Asian Americans, and whites, with Hispanics enrolled at only about half the rates of the others. This latter result is a curious one, but seems consistent with a generally lower use of Catholic schools by Hispanics than would be predicted by their religious affiliation. This effect may be due to the lack of a private school tradition in the Latin American countries from which the Hispanic minorities emigrated. On the other hand, it seems clear that African Americans, Asian Americans, and whites who are Catholic do make use of Catholic schools at about the same rate (about 20%), despite the lower income levels of the African Americans.

The results for students from different parents' education backgrounds show that the existing difference between the enrollment rates (Column 1) is hardly reduced by estimating the proportions of those attending religious private schools if all the members were Catholic. The difference becomes greater rather than less.

Standardizing for Income

Unlike public school choice, the constraints on private school choice include financial cost as well as availability of a private school. Because the proportion attending a private school is so small, the method of standardizing for opportunity used in choice of public schools earlier in the paper is not feasible nor appropriate. What is appropriate is to standardize by financial opportunity. This can best be done by examining enrollment in private school at the 8th grade, rather than proportion considering private high school, because it is in actual enrollment that the income constraints have an effect.[10] This can be done in a similar manner to public school choice by using logistic regressions modeling enrollment in either religious or non-religious private schools versus not enrolling in them. Calculation of predicted enrollments if income were standardized to the population average is as described in equations (9) through (11) in Appendix 6.1, but with release of income constraints rather than constraints on opportunity for choice. Standardizing enrollments to the all-student average allows estimation of relative enrollment rates if income constraints were relaxed. Table 6.8 shows the existing levels of enrollment in religious schools (in Column 1), and the enrollment when the group's income is standardized to the average for all students (Column 2). Column 2 shows that the

TABLE 6.8 Actual enrollments in religious schools, and enrollments standardized for each group to the income average for all students of $38,353[11]

	(1) Actual proportion enrolled	(2) Enrollment standardized To all-student income average
Race/Ethnicity		
African American	.052	.052
Asian American	.126	.116
Hispanic	.089	.092
White	.110	.109
Parents' education		
High school	.056	.058
Some college	.096	.097
College or more	.159	.154

TABLE 6.9 Actual enrollments in non-religious schools, and enrollments standardized for each group to the income average for all students of $38,390[12]

	(1) Actual proportion enrolled	(2) Enrollment standardized to all-student income average
Race/Ethnicity		
African American	.005	.005
Asian American	.031	.020
Hispanic	.004	.003
White	.017	.012
Parents' education		
High school	.002	.002
Some college	.007	.006
College or more	.045	.028

enrollment standardized to a common income reduces slightly the differences between Asian Americans, Hispanics, and whites. There remains, however, a large difference in enrollment between African Americans and the others, who are at twice the African American level. The groups classified by parents' education show small reductions in the enrollment differences when incomes are standardized.

Table 6.9 shows comparable figures for non-religious private schools. Column 1 shows actual enrollments, and Column 2 shows enrollments standardized to the all-student income average. These enrollments rates are, as Table 6.6 showed, a minuscule part of the overall school enrollment for all groups. But, as will be evident from the table, the pattern among groups is quite different from that for religiously-based schools. As Column 2 shows, both for racial and ethnic groups and for parents' education groups, those groups with higher average income show some reduction of enrollment when incomes are standardized at the all-student average. But, African Americans, Hispanics, and low or medium parent-education groups show no increase in enrollment in non-religious private schools.

Comparing the responsiveness to relaxation of income constraints for groups differing in parents' education shows a pattern on the part of the highly educated parents similar to that of whites. Comparing this with Table 6.8 suggests the same tendency conjectured for whites: to substitute non-religious private schools for religious private schools as income increases.

Other Indicators of Response to Increased Opportunity

The results of the previous sections give some indication of the effect of expansion of choice on inequality through expansion of choice in the public sector or eliminating tuition costs of private schooling. There are other indicators, perhaps less direct than the above, but giving another indication of possible impact of expansion of choice on inequality. NELS:88 provides some evidence of the involvement of parents in their children's education, and thus their likely response to increased educational opportunity in the form of expanded choice of school. Parents' reports of expenditures on various kinds of education outside school is one such type of information. Parents were asked about instruction in art, music, dance, history, religious and computer classes, and tutoring. Although these extra classes have various purposes, expenditures on tutoring and on computer classes appeared to be fairly direct measures of the parents' implementation of an interest in educational achievement. The proportion of parents having their child tutored outside school is quite small, only .043 for the cohort as a whole. The proportion taking computer classes is higher, .108. Like private school enrollment, both of these activities will be examined for the racial and ethnic groups, and for the parents' education groups.

Table 6.10 shows the current proportion of parents who were making expenditures on tutoring, by racial/ethnic and parents' education groups, and the proportions that would be expected to do so if all the students in each group had the same income as the average for all students. The current proportion using outside tutoring shows a very high gradient by parents' education, with those having a college degree more than five times as likely to have their child in outside tutoring than those with no more than a high school education. The racial and ethnic differences are considerably less. Asian Americans are highest, whites intermediate, and African Americans and Hispanics lowest.

When income is standardized at the average level of all students (but all students keeping their own background characteristics, so that the only

TABLE 6.10 Proportion of parents making expenditures on tutoring outside school for their child, and predicted proportion if average income for the group were equal to the average for all students, by racial/ethnic groups and by parents' education[13]

	Proportion spending on tutoring	Predicted proportion spending on tutoring if income were at average for all students
Race/Ethnicity		
African American	.034	.036
Asian American	.073	.056
Hispanic	.026	.027
White	.046	.039
Parents' education		
High school	.016	.018
Some college	.037	.037
College or more	.086	.061

change is in income) the predicted proportion paying a tutor is given in the right hand column. These numbers show a reduced, but still quite large, gradient for parents' education groups. The 5:1 ratio for the extremes has been reduced, but only to about 3:1. For racial and ethnic groups, the differences between whites, African Americans, and Hispanics have essentially vanished, and only the Asian Americans show a substantially greater proportion using tutors. Thus by this measure, less well educated parents exhibit lesser interest in their children's educational achievement than do better educated parents, a deficiency which is not simply due to their lower income. For racial and ethnic minorities, this is not true: Although their overall levels of having children tutored outside school are lower than that of whites (except for Asian Americans, whose level is higher), this is accounted for by their lower income. Even though their average education is lower and they have other characteristics (such as larger families) which would lead to lower use of tutoring, their use of tutors when income is taken into consideration is not lower.

Enrollment of their 8th grade child in computer classes outside school is another measure of parents' interest in their children's educational achievement. Table 6.10 shows the proportions of children in each racial and ethnic group and in each parental education group who are enrolled in computer classes. The table also shows, in the right hand column, the enrollment when income is standardized at the level of all students. Again, the other background characteristics are unchanged, so that the only equalization is in family income to reduce or eliminate difference due to ability to afford such classes.

Table 6.11 shows a pattern of results similar to that of Table 6.10. Parents with a college degree are three times as likely to have their children in

TABLE 6.11 Proportion of parents making expenditures on computer classes for their child, and predicted proportion if average income for the group were equal to the average for all students by racial/ethnic groups and by parents' education[14]

	Proportion spending on computer classes	Predicted proportion spending on computer classes if income were at average for all students
Race/Ethnicity		
African American	.114	.117
Asian American	.160	.161
Hispanic	.076	.081
White	.110	.108
Parents' education		
High school	.054	.056
Some college	.105	.107
College or more	.177	.168

computer classes as are those with only a high school education. This ratio is hardly reduced when standardized by income. For racial and ethnic groups, Asian Americans are again highest. Here, African Americans and whites are about the same, and only Hispanics are lower. After standardizing on income, Asian American levels are unaffected, while the other three groups are African Americans, whites, and Hispanics in that order. Only the difference between Asian Americans and the others, and Hispanics and the others, are almost certain to be true in the population. (See footnote to Table 6.2 for rules of thumb on statistical significance.)

The inferences about underlying processes are like those made for the tutoring classes. The less well educated parents again show less interest in their child's achievement than do better educated parents, which is not accounted for by lower income. Among racial and ethnic groups, Asian Americans exhibit greatest interest in their children's education by this measure, while African Americans exhibit at least as much as whites, despite their lower educational levels. Hispanic parents by this measure show the least interest in their child's educational achievement.

Another indicator of parents' implementation of an interest in their child's education is saving for further education. Overall, close to half of all parents expecting their student to attend college reported having saved money for their child's education. The percentage of parents in each racial-ethnic group and in each parents' education group who report savings for their child's education is given in Table 6.12. These percentages are all high; this is an activity which covers more than a small minority in each group, as was true both for tutoring and for computer classes. Thus more

TABLE 6.12 Proportion of parents expecting their student to attend college reporting having saved money for their child's further education, and predicted proportion if average income for the group were equal to the average for all students ($40,310) by racial/ethnic groups and by parents' education[15]

	Proportion having saved	Predicted proportion saving if income were at average for all students
Race/Ethnicity		
African American	.421	.506
Asian American	.621	.609
Hispanic	.372	.442
White	.516	.509
Parents' education		
High school	.335	.404
Some college	.469	.498
College or more	.669	.636

confidence can be placed in results concerning saving for college reflecting the behavior of the group as a whole.

The parents' education groups show large differences in the percent having saved money for their child's further education; the racial and ethnic groups also show differences but they are somewhat smaller. The patterns are similar to those expenditures on tutoring and on computer classes.

When these proportions are standardized to the average family income for all students, the parents' education differences decline only slightly, and remain substantial. The differences are less great for the racial and ethnic groups. Asian Americans are again highest and Hispanics lowest, with African Americans and whites in between.

The results of this examination of investments outside school and savings for further education are quite consistent over the three kinds of activities. There is a high gradient of investment with increase in parents' education, ranging from college-graduate parents being twice as likely to save for further education, compared to parents with only a high school education, to being five times as likely to make expenditures on tutoring. These disproportionate investments would be predicted to be somewhat less if incomes among the educational groups were alike, but not greatly less. Parents' education *per se* appears to be an important factor in responsiveness to educational opportunities for their children.

Racial and ethnic groups show much less difference in investments of these three types. There are differences, with Asian Americans being consistently highest. The predicted proportions making investments if incomes were equalized, eliminating differences in cost constraints, are closer but Asian Americans remain highest. Hispanics remain lowest. However, the proportion of African Americans making investments is predicted to be just about the same as the proportion of whites.

The results from money spent on tutoring, computer classes, and savings for college show two different patterns. As in earlier analyses, the differences between two kinds of disadvantage become apparent, one evident in the actions of the racial and ethnic minorities, and the other evident in the actions of the different parents' education groups. For the racial and ethnic groups, the effect of disadvantage on parents' investments in their children's education appears to be primarily through lack of resources. The only difference that is not primarily due to resources is that between the higher investments of Asian Americans than of other groups. The differences in investments between minorities and whites are small (in the case of African Americans and Hispanics), or in favor of the minority groups (for Asian Americans, whose financial resources are as high as those of whites). When financial resources are equated, the differences vanish for African Americans and become small for Hispanics. The evidence indicates that elimination of financial constraints would, for these minorities, sharply reduce inequality of educational opportunity for their children.

For students differing in parents' education, the effects of disadvantage from their parents' investment in their education appear to be deeper than mere absence of financial resources. The differences are large as they stand, and when the groups are equated on financial resources, the differences do not vanish, but are only slightly reduced. The indication is that for this form of disadvantage, elimination of financial constraints would not eliminate or sharply reduce inequality of educational opportunity for their children.

What Does One Make of All This?

The analysis in the pages above give an indication of the potential impact of expansion of school choice on inequality of educational opportunity. There are cogent *a priori* arguments given in an earlier section of the chapter to support either the belief that this would increase inequality or the belief that it would decrease inequality. The belief that it would increase inequality rests on the argument that parents in the more advantaged families would, because of their greater knowledge of the educational system, be more likely to take advantage of choice as well as make other investments in their children, who thus would benefit more than would disadvantaged children. The latter would be left behind in the most deficient schools. The opposite belief, that choice would decrease inequality, rests on the argument that the most disadvantaged have the most constraints on choice, for they are most constrained to live in poverty and ghetto areas of central cities. They would gain most because the current system of school assignment by residence is most harmful to them.

The results of the analysis show a more complex pattern than either of these two positions. Three major generalizations seem possible from these results.

First, minority or immigrant status appears to bring a special responsiveness to opportunity for choice in education that is not apparent among whites of comparable backgrounds. Students from African American and Hispanic backgrounds, although quite disadvantaged in terms of income and parents' education, showed strong response to opportunities for choice in the public sector and in the religious private sector, and are making educational investments outside school that are quite beyond the average for their income and parental education levels. Asian Americans, with minority status although advantaged in income and parents' education relative to the student average, are higher than any other group on all these indicators of responsiveness to expanded parental choice.

The special responsiveness of minority and immigrant groups becomes especially apparent when a different dimension of disadvantage is examined, that is, parents' lack of education. Children from the least well-educated parents (the great majority of whom are whites, even though proportions are higher among African Americans and Hispanics) show the least responsiveness to almost every form of opportunity for choice or investment in their children's education. Of all the groups they appear best characterized by the first argument stated at the outset, that expansion of educational opportunity through choice would increase inequality because the most disadvantaged would be least likely to respond to the increased opportunity.[16] What is especially striking is that disadvantaged racial and ethnic minorities, although the parents have low levels of education, do not show this same lack of response to increased opportunity.

Second, the pattern of response to expanded opportunity for choice is very different among different groups. African Americans and Hispanics show a pattern in which response is primarily within the public sector, then in the religious private sector, and very little in the non-religious private sector. The African American exercise of choice among public-sector schools is especially pronounced—both in the actual frequency with which more than one high school was considered (Table 6.2) and in the high response in those school settings where the opportunity for choice is high (Table 6.4). Whites show by far the least exercise of choice in the public sector (in part due to rural residence or to having exercised public school choice through choice of residence, primarily in suburbs), and, as income increases, are less likely to make use of religious than non-religious schools. Asian Americans show a pattern all their own. This includes a special affinity for private schools and in educational investments outside school. This may be due to their anomalous position of racial minority status, combined with higher education and income than average. They show highest enrollment in both religious and non-religious sectors (Table 6.6), their estimated rise in enrollment in both sectors with increase in income is higher than those of other groups (Tables 6.7 and 6.8). Among those in public schools at the 8th grade level, they are also most likely to consider a private high school. This pattern may be a result of their being somewhat more constrained in choice of residence than are whites, and thus less often able to exercise their educational choice through choice of residence.

Third, the investments in education outside school through computer classes, tutors, and savings for college provide additional evidence of the special responsiveness of minority and immigrant groups to increase in educational opportunity. The difference between racial and ethnic minorities on one hand and students disadvantaged by low parental education on the other suggests, as indicated earlier, a deeper form of disadvantage for the educationally disadvantaged than for the racially or ethnically disadvantaged. The latter groups appear disadvantaged in external resources, but relatively responsive once those resources are available. The former appear disadvantaged in internal resources, less likely to respond to opportunities that become available.

Notes

1. From *Digest of Education Statistics: 1989* (25th edition). Washington, D.C.: U.S. Department of Education.

2. The median family income in the United States in 1988 was $30,853 (from *Statistical Abstract of the United States: 1990* (110th edition). Washington, D.C.: U.S. Bureau of the Census).

3. Minnesota adopted the inter-district choice policy by legislation, beginning in the school year 1990-91, and a number of other states are beginning or considering a similar policy.

4. The question arises concerning what inferences about the population may be made from the sample estimates in the table. The effective sample sizes (corrected for the design effect) for the proportion of persons considering more than one high school (column 1) are as follows: African Americans, 1450; Asian Americans, 240; Hispanics, 900; whites, 8100; low education, 3600; medium education, 5100; high education, 2800. As a conservative rule of thumb, the differences between proportions of actual choice are statistically significant at the 5% level for: (a) differences of .060 in all comparisons involving Asian Americans; (b) differences of .035 in all other comparisons involving Hispanics; (c) differences of .030 in comparisons of African Americans with whites; (d) differences of .020 in education comparisons involving the high education group; (e) differences of .015 in comparisons between the other two education groups.

5. Asian American students are not included because the number in the low-educated category is small. Even if they were present in a sufficient number for analysis, the differences between those with low education and those with high education get confounded by differences in time of immigration and country of origin. Separating these factors out would complicate the analysis and lower the reliability.

6. See Appendix 6.1 for a description of the procedures for calculating these estimates.

7. Standardization by opportunity is based on a logistic regression equation in which the following background characteristics of each group were statistically controlled: student's gender, parents' education, family income, mother-father family structure, number of siblings, Catholic religion, parents' expectations for child's education, and (for the education groups) racial or ethnic group. See Appendix 6.1 for explanation of calculations. Because this is a nonlinear regression, the predicted proportions must be calculated for each individual and then averaged. Thus the right-hand column of the table cannot be calculated from a table of logistic regression coefficients and group means. In the case of non-linearity, the average of individual changes is not given by changing the overall average via use of regression coefficients.

8. An examination of the types of public high schools NELS:88 students ended up attending, drawing on the 1990 First Follow-up data, indicated that those students considering more than two public high schools were more likely to end up in "public schools of choice" and high schools in districts allowing easy transfers.

9. Standardization to 100% Catholic is based on logistic regression equations in which the following background characteristics of each group were statistically controlled: student's gender, number of siblings, Catholic religion, Northeast region, rural residence, mother-father family structure, parents' expectations for child's education, parents' education, and (for the educational groups) racial and ethnic-group.

10. For proportions considering private high school (Column 1 in Table 6.6), there is very little effect of income. Standardizing the racial and ethnic groups by income to the average for all students would increase Hispanics from .034 to .039 and reduce Asian Americans from .058 to .054, but would have virtually no effect on whites and African Americans.

11. Standardization by income is based on logistic regression equations in which the following background characteristics of each group were statistically controlled: student's gender, number of siblings, Catholic religion, Northeast region, rural residence, mother-father family structure, parents' expectations for child's education, parents' education, and (for the educational groups) racial and ethnic-group.

12. The non-linearity of logistic regression models produces unexpected standardized proportions (Column 3) of enrollment in non-religious private schools for African Americans, Hispanics, and students whose parents have attended only high school. Because the actual proportions of students in these groups enrolling in non-religious private schools is so small (under .01), we are modeling the extreme end of the logistic regression function, which is curved. With ordinary least squares regression (OLS) models we would expect standardization to show an increase in the mean probability that a student would enroll in a non-religious

private school because these groups have average incomes below the overall mean and income is positively related to enrollment. However, this is not necessarily true with logistic regression functions, which are multiplicative not linear. When estimating standardized enrollment probabilities using logistic regression models, the likelihood of enrollment for students above the overall mean income might be reduced more per dollar than the likelihood is increased per dollar for those below the overall mean. As a result, the average decrease in the first group may be larger than or equal to the average increase of the second.

13. Standardization by income is based on logistic regression equations in which the following background characteristics of each groups were statistically controlled: student's gender, number of siblings, Catholic religion, Northeast region, rural residence, mother-father family structure, parents' expectations for child's education, parents' education, and (for the educational groups) racial or ethnic-group.

14. Standardization by income is based on logistic regression equations in which the following background characteristics of each groups were statistically controlled: student's gender, number of siblings, Catholic religion, Northeast region, rural residence, mother-father family structure, parents' expectations for child's college, parents' education, and (for the educational groups) racial or ethnic group.

15. Standardization by income is based on logistic regression equations in which the following background characteristics of each groups were statistically controlled: student's gender, number of siblings, Catholic religion, Northeast region, rural residence, mother-father family structure, parents' expectations for child's education, parents' education, and (for the educational groups) racial or ethnic group.

16. A portion of the lower response of the least well-educated lies in their disproportionate rural residence, a factor that has not been considered in the analysis.

Appendix 6.1

The separation of constraints on public school choice that are alike for all students in the same school from the differential tendency of students from different social backgrounds to consider more than one public high school can be carried out as follows:

Let s = number of schools

n_j = number of students in school j who name one public school or two public schools (categories 1 and 3 below)

$n = \sum_{j=1}^{s} n_j$ = total number of students in categories 1 and 3.

The measure of choice is, as indicated in the text, based on the number and sector of high schools named as high schools that might be attended. Eighth grade students were classified into five categories:

1. Those considering one public high school
2. Those considering one private high school
3. Those considering two public high schools
4. Those considering one public high school and one private high school
5. Those considering two private high schools.

For public school choice, a categorical variable y_{ij} is created, using those in category 1 and those in category 3.

y_{ij} = 1 if two public high schools are being considered by student i (category 3); = 0 if only one public school is being considered (category 1)

$$m = \sum_{j=1}^{s} \sum_{i=1}^{n_j} y_{ij}$$
= number of students considering two schools

X_{ij} = a vector of demographic characteristics of student i that best predict y_{ij} with $X_{o\,ij} = 1$.

(Characteristics of the student that are predictors of choice and are not influenced by the opportunities for choice are included. Those social characteristics, such as race/ethnicity and parents' education, for which the tendency to exercise choice will be measured are included.)

In a logistic regression of y on X, we find the vector B which minimizes the sum of squared errors, e_{ij} in eq. (1):

$$\log \frac{y_{ij}}{1-y_{ij}} = BX_{ij} + e_{ij} \tag{1}$$

The predicted value of y_{ij}, y_{ij}^*, is given by

$$y_{ij}^* = \frac{1}{1 + \exp(BX_{ij})} \tag{2}$$

The quantity y_{ij}^* is the predicted probability that student i in school j names more than one school.

Then for student h in school j, it is possible to calculate both the expected and the actual proportion of students in that school who were exercising public school choice.

The actual proportion is

$$y_{hj} = \frac{1}{n_j - 1} \sum_{\substack{i=1 \\ i \neq h}}^{n_j} y_{ij} \tag{3}$$

The expected proportion is

$$y_{hj}^* = \frac{1}{n_j - 1} \sum_{\substack{i=1 \\ i \neq h}}^{n_j} y_{ij}^* \tag{4}$$

The difference, $y_{hj} - y_{hj}^*$, between the actual number choosing and the expected number choosing is a measure of the extra or deficient opportunity for choice in school j, independent of the action of student h. Then the opportunity for choice in school j as estimated for student h is given by the overall proportion of choice, m/n, plus this deviation from expected in school j:

$$d_{hj} = \frac{m}{n} + (y_{hj} - y_{hj}^*) \tag{5}$$

The average opportunity for choice for all students of a particular racial/ethnic or educational background is obtained by finding the average of d_{hj} over all students h with background k. First, define δ_{hjk} as 1 if student h in school j is in group k and 0 otherwise. Then the average opportunity for students from background k, d_k, is given by

$$d_k = \frac{\sum\limits_{j=1}^{s} \sum\limits_{h=1}^{n_j} d_{jh} \, \delta_{hjk}}{\sum\limits_{j=1}^{s} \sum\limits_{h=1}^{n_j} \delta_{hjk}} \qquad (6)$$

where d_k is the average opportunity for students from background k to consider more than one school, based on the proportion of students in their schools who consider more than one public high school, standardized by student body characteristics.

Then it is possible to determine the added or deficient proportion of students from different social backgrounds (that is different racial and ethnic backgrounds or different educational levels) who are considering more than one high school, relative to the opportunity in the school, by the following calculations:

$$c_k = \frac{\sum\limits_{j=1}^{s} \sum\limits_{i=1}^{n_j} y_{hj} \, \delta_{hjk}}{\sum\limits_{j=1}^{s} \sum\limits_{h=1}^{n_j} \delta_{hjk}} \qquad (7)$$

where c_k is the proportion of students with background k who consider more than one school.

Then $c_k - d_k$ is the additional or deficient probability of students from background k to exercise choice, relative to the opportunity in their schools, and

$$r_k = c_k - d_k + \frac{m}{n} \qquad (8)$$

is the probability of students from background k to exercise choice (i.e., consider more than one school), standardized for the opportunity provided by the schools they are in.

The quantity r_k gives a measure of the existing choice probability for students from background k, standardized for the schools they are in, which are themselves standardized for the propensity of students in those schools to exercise choice. Comparison of these quantities between groups k and k' indicates the relative responsiveness of groups k and k' to the existing opportunities for choice. It does not, however, show what the responsiveness of these groups to expanded choice would be, as would occur if public school choice were universal.

An estimate of the responsiveness of group k to expanded choice can be obtained by regressing y_{hj} on d_{hj} for all members of group k. Because d_{hj} may be correlated with characteristics of students that have high or low probabilities of exercising choice, it is necessary to statistically control on these characteristics by including them in the regression equation. All the characteristics in vector X_{ij} other than the background characteristics under consideration (race or ethnicity, education) are included. The regression coefficient of d_{hj} for group k shows the rate at which the probability that a person in group k will exercise choice increases as the opportunity for choice increases.

If y_{hj} were normally distributed, then ordinary least squares regression could be used to obtain an estimate of the proportion of students in group k who would consider more than one high school if public school choice were expanded. The estimate could be found by augmenting the current proportion of students in group k who exercise choice by the proportion who would be expected to do so (based on the regression coefficient on d_{hj} in the equation for group k) if the opportunity d_{hj} were increased to some high and standard level, say d*.

However, this method cannot be used when y_{ij} is a categorical variable taking on only values of 0 or 1, as in this case. Logistic regression, as in equation (1), must be used. Because the predicted value of y_{ij} is not a linear function of the independent variables, it is necessary to first carry out the logistic regression, separately for each group k, then calculate for each individual the expected value of y_{ij} when the opportunity for choice is augmented to d*, and finally find the mean of these expected values over all students in group k. This gives the expected proportions of students in group k who would exercise choice if the opportunities for choice were expanded to a level expressed by d*.

Expressed mathematically, this involves logistic regression analysis for each racial/ethnic or education group, where the equation for student h in school j is:

$$\log \frac{y_{hi}}{1 - y_{hi}} = BX_{hj} + b_d d_{jh} + e_{hj} \qquad (9)$$

where

X_{ij} is a vector of background characteristics,

d_{jh} is the opportunity for choice for student h in school j, as calculated in equation (5),

b_d is a coefficient which estimates the change in $\log [y_{hj}/(1 - y_{hj})]$ with change in d_{hj}.

Then the expected probability of exercising choice for student h in school j when the opportunity for choice is not d_{hj} but d* is given by

$$y_{hi}{}^+ = \frac{1}{\exp[BX_{hj} + b_d(d* - d_{jh})]} \qquad (10)$$

Seven regression equations are estimated, one each for African Americans, Asian Americans, Hispanics, whites, parents' education, (high school only, some college, and college degree). For each, the expected proportion exercising choice is

$$C_k{}^* = \sum_{j=1}^{s} \sum_{h=1}^{n_{jk}} y_{hj}{}^+ \qquad (11)$$

where n_{jk} = the number of students of group k in school j, and h is an index from 1 to n_{jk} for students of group k in school j. The values of $C_k{}^*$ are given in Column 3 of Table 6.4.

The quantities shown in Tables 1-5 are:

Table 6.1:	Column 1:	d_k
Table 6.2:	Column 1:	c_k
	Column 2:	d_k
	Column 3:	$c_k - d_k$
	Column 4:	r_k
Table 6.3:	Column 1:	c_k
	Column 2:	r_k
Table 6.4:	Column 1:	c_k
	Column 2:	$c_k{}^*$
Table 6.5:	Column 1:	c_k

Appendix 6.2

The analysis in this chapter is based on a sample which excludes Native Americans and students in schools where more than 33% of the students attend remedial reading classes. The standardized sampling weights used in this analysis are the same as those used in other chapters: BYQWT for each student divided by the mean of the weights for the entire NELS:88 data set (without excluding any cases). In addition, t-values for regression coefficients were divided by a conservative design effect of 1.56.

The variables and their sources on the NELS:88 public use file are:

- **Male:** SEX in the composite variable section of the student file recoded so that "male" = 1 and "female" = 0.

- **Parents' Education:** The highest value from either BYP30 or BYP31 from the parent questionnaire were the first reference for this variable. If both were missing, the highest value from either BYS34A or BYS34B was used. The resulting variable was coded as follows: "did not finish high school" = 0; "high school graduate or G.E.D." = 1; "Less than 2 years beyond high school" = 2; "2 or more years beyond high school" = 3; "finished a 4 or 5 year program" = 4; "Master's or similar degree" = 6; "Ph.D. or other advanced degree" = 8.

- **Income/$10,000:** Taken from BYP80 in parent file recoded to the mid-point for each category (i.e., "$1,000 to $2,999" = 2000, and "$100,000 to $199,999" = 150000). The values were then divided by 10000.

- **Step-Parent, Single Parent, Other Family, Two-Natural Parents:** Taken from BYFCOMP in the composite variable section of the student file with the following recodes: "mother and male guardian" and "father and female guardian" coded as "step-parent family"; "mother only" and "father only" coded as "single parent"; and "other relative or non-relative" coded as "other family." If the information in BYFCOMP was designated "missing", information from BYP1A1 and BYP1A2 was used to construct similar categories. Once a composite "family composition" variable was constructed, indicators variables were created with a designated family type coded as 1 and otherwise categories equal to 0.

- **Number of Sibs:** BYP3B from the parent file was used as the first reference. If a value for that variable was missing, BYS32 from the student file was used. If both were missing values, then one sibling was counted for each item marked in BYS8E and BYS8F from the student file as a final source.

- **Catholic:** BYP29 in the parent file recoded so that "Catholic" = 1 and any other category = 0.

- **Parent Expectations:** BYP76 from the parent file was used as the first reference, supplemented by BYS48A and BYS48B from the student file if values from the first variable were missing. The resulting variable was coded as follows: "will not finish high school" = 0; "graduate high school" = 1; "trade school" = 2; "some college" = 3; "finished a 4 or 5 year program" = 4; "attend graduate school" = 6.

- **African Americans, Asian Americans, Hispanics:** A variable for parental race was constructed using BYP10 in the parent file as the first reference, supplemented by RACE from the composite variable section of the student file if the parent information was missing. Indicator variables were constructed from the composite variable with the designated race = 1 and otherwise = 0.

- **Northeast Area:** Taken from G8REGON in the composite variable section of the student file and recoded so that "Northeast - New England and Middle Atlantic states" = 1 and other categories = 0.

- **Rural Location:** Taken from G8URBAN in the composite variable section of the student file and recoded so that "Rural" = 1, and "Urban" and "Suburban" = 0.

- **Public Choice:** This variable was constructed for public school eighth graders who are considering only public high schools using BYS14, BYS15, and BYS16. Students who answered "public" on BYS14 but either answered "No" on BYS15 or did not answer either BYS15 or BYS16 were coded as 0. Students who answered "public" on BYS14 and either answered "Yes" on BYS15 or "public" on BYS16 were coded as 1.

- **Private Choice:** This variable was constructed for public school eighth graders in a similar manner to "Public Choice" using BYS14, BYS15, and BYS16. Students who have either 0 or 1 on "Public Choice" were coded as 0. Students who answered either "private" on BYS14 or "private" on BYS16 were coded as 1.

- **Religious Private, Non-Religious Private:** A school type variable was constructed using G8CTRL from the composite variable section of the student file and with "Catholic" and "Other Religious" coded as "Religious Private." Indicator variables were constructed in which the designated school type = 1 and other categories = 0.

References

Astone, Nan Marie, and Sara S. McLanahan. 1991. "Family structure, parental practices and high school completion." *American Sociological Review* 56: 309-320.

Baker, D. P., and D. L. Stevenson. 1986. "Mother's Strategies for Children's School Achievement: Managing the Transition to High School." *Sociology of Education* 59:156-167.

Baumrind, D. 1973. "The Development of Instrumental Competence Through Socialization." In *Minnesota Symposium on Child Psychology*, vol. 7, ed. A. D. Pick. Minneapolis: University of Minnesota Press.

Becker, H. J., and J. L. Epstein. 1982. "Parent Involvement: A Survey of Teacher Practices." *Elementary School Journal* 83:85-102.

Berger, E. H. 1991. *Parents as Partners in Education*. New York: Merrill.

Brandt, R. S. 1979. *Partner: Parents and Schools*. Alexandria: Association of Supervision and Curriculum Development.

Bryk, A., and S. Raudenbush. 1992. *Hierarchical Linear Models: Applications and Data Analysis Methods*. Newbury Park, Calif.: Sage Publications.

Bumpass, Larry. 1984. "Children and Marital Disruption: A Replication and Update." *Demography* 21: 71-82.

Burstein, L. 1980. "The Analysis of Multi-level Data in Educational Research and Evaluation." *Review of Research in Education* 8:158-233.

Caldwell, B. M., and R. H. Bradley. 1984. *Home Observation for Measurement of the Environment*. Little Rock, Arkansas: University of Arkansas.

Clark, Reginald M. 1983. *Family Life and School Achievement: Why Poor Black Children Succeed or Fail*. Chicago: University of Chicago.

Clifton, Rodney A. et al. 1986. "Effects of Ethnicity and Sex on Teachers' Expectations of Junior High School Students." *Sociology of Education* 59: 58-67.

Coleman, J. S. 1987. "Families and schools". *Educational Researcher* 16 (6): 32-38.

Coleman, J. S. 1988. "Social Capital in the Creation of Human Capital." *American Journal of Sociology* 94: S95-S120.

Coleman, J. S. 1990. *Foundations of Social Theory*. Cambridge, Mass.: Belknap Press of Harvard University Press.

Coleman, J. S. et al. 1987. Analysis of National Education Longitudinal Studies Data: Scientific Proposal Submitted by NORC. NORC, Chicago.

Coleman, J. S., E. Q. Campbell, C. J. Hobson, J. McPartland, A. M. Mood, F. D. Weinfeld, and R. L. York. 1966. *Equality of Educational Opportunity*. Washington, D.C.: U.S. Government Printing Office.

Coleman, J. S., and T. Hoffer. 1987. *Public and Private Schools: The Impact of Communities*. New York: Basic Books.

Coleman, J. S., T. Hoffer, and S. Kilgore. 1982. *High School Achievement: Public, Catholic, and Private Schools Compared.* New York: Basic Books.

Corwin, R. G., and T. C. Wagenaar. 1976. "Boundary Interaction between Service Organizations and Their Publics: A Study of Teacher-Parent Relationships." *Social Forces* 55:471-92.

Diprete, Thomas A. 1981. Discipline and Order in American High School. Report to the National Center for Education Statistics. NORC, Chicago.

Dornbusch, Sanford M., et al. 1985. "Single Parents, Extended Households, and the Control of Adolescents." *Child Development* 56: 326-341.

Dornbusch, S. M., P. L. Ritter, P. H. Leiderman, D. F. Roberts, and M. J. Fraleigh. 1987. "The Relation of Parenting Style to Adolescent School Performance." *Child Development* 58:1244-1257.

Epstein, J.L. 1987. "Toward a Theory of Family-School Connections: Teacher Practices and Parent Involvement across the School Years." In *Social Intervention: Potential and Constraints,* ed. K. Hurrelmann, F. Kaufmann, and F. Losel. New York: de Gruyter.

Epstein, J. L. 1990 "Single Parents and the Schools: Effects of Marital Status on Parent and Teacher Interactions." In *Change in Societal Institutions,* ed. Maureen T. Hallinan, David M. Klein, and Jennifer Glass. New York: Plenum Press.

Epstein, J. L. 1991. "Effects on Student Achievement of Teachers' Practices of Parent Involvement." In *Advances in Readings/Language Research,* ed. Steven B. Silvern. Greenwich, Connecticut: JAI Press.

Epstein, J.L., and H. J. Becker. 1982. "Teachers' Reported Practices of Parent Involvement: Problems and Possibilities." *Elementary School Journal* 55:103- 113.

Erbe, B., et al. 1990. "Parent Participation Programs in the Chicago Public Schools." *Typescript,* Roosevelt University, December.

Fehrmann, P. G., T. Z. Keith, and T. M. Reimers. 1987. "Home Influence on School Learning: Direct and Indirect Effects of Parental Involvement on High School Grades." *Journal of Educational Research* 80:330-337.

Garfinkel, Irwin, and Sara S. McLanahan. 1986. *Single Mothers and Their Children.* Washington, DC: Urban Institute Press.

Goldberger, A. S., and G. G. Cain. 1982. "The Causal Analysis of Cognitive Outcomes in the Coleman, Hoffer, and Kilgore Report." *Sociology of Education* 55:103-22.

Heyns, B. 1978. *Summer Learning and the Effects of Schooling.* New York: Academic Press.

Hoover-Dempsey, V., O. C. Bassler, and J. S. Brissie. 1987. "Parent Involvement: Contributions of Teacher Efficacy, School Socio-economic Status, and Other School Characteristics." *American Educational Research Journal* 24:417-35.

Jencks, C., et al. 1972. *Inequality: A Reassessment of the Effects of Family Schooling in America.* New York: Basic Books.

Landerholm, E. 1988. "Survey of Parent Involvement Program Activities Offered at Early Intervention Centers in a Seven Stat Area." *ICEC Quarterly* 37:24-29.

Lareau, A. 1987. "Social Class Differences in Family-School Relationships: The Importance of Cultural Capital." *Sociology of Education* 60:73-85.

Lareau, A. 1989. *Home Advantage: Social Class and Parental Intervention in Elementary Education.* London: Falmer Press.

Leichter, Hope. 1978. "Families and Communities as Educators: Some Concepts of Relationship." *Teachers College Record* 79:567-658.

Litwak, E., and H. J. Meyer. 1974. *School, Family, and Neighborhood: The Theory and Practice of School-Community Relations.* New York: Columbia University Press.

Marjoribanks, K. 1979. *Families and Their Learning Environments.* London: Routledge & Kegan Paul.

Mason, W., G. Wong, and B. Entwistle. 1983. "Contextual Analysis through the Multilevel Linear Model." In *Sociological Methodology 1983-1984*, ed. S. Leinhart, 72-103. San Francisco: Jossey-Bass.

Milne, Ann M., et al. 1986. "Single Parents, Working Mothers, and the Educational Achievement of School Children." *Sociology of Education* 59: 125-139.

Moles, Oliver C. 1992. "School Performance of Children from One-Parent Families." In *Changing Lives: Studies in Human Development and Professional Helping*, ed. Martin Bloom. Columbia, S.C.: University of South Carolina Press.

Muller, C., K. Schiller, and S.A. Lee. 1991. "Defying Statistics: (or "Latch-key Children in the Late '80s:") Family Composition, Working Mothers, and After School Supervision." Paper presented at the Annual Meeting of the American Educational Research Association, Chicago, Illinois.

Muller, C. 1991. Parental Involvement in the Education Process: An Analysis of Family Resources and Academic Achievement. Ph.D. diss., University of Chicago.

Pallas, Aaron M.,, et al. 1989. "The Changing Nature of the Disadvantaged Population: Current Dimensions and Future Trends." *Educational Researcher* 18 (5):16-22.

Pink, W. T. 1987. "In Search of Exemplary Junior High Schools: A Case Study." In *Schooling in Social Context: Qualitative Studies*, ed. G. Noblit and W. T. Pink. Norwood, N. J.: Ablex.

Powell, D. R. 1978. "Correlates of Parent-Teacher Communication Frequency and Diversity." *Journal of Educational Research* 71:333-41.

Rumberger, Russell W., et al. 1990. "Family Influences on Dropout Behavior in One California High School." *Sociology of Education* 63: 283-299.

Rumberger, R.W., R. Ghatak, G. Poulos, P. L. Ritter, and S.M. Dornbusch. 1990. "Family Influences on Dropout Behavior in One California High School." *Sociology of Education* 63:283-299.

Schneider, Barbara, J. Hieshima, and S. A. Lee. 1991. "East Asian Academic Success: Family, School, and Community Explanations," In *The Development of the Minority Child: Culture In and Out of Context.* ed. P. Greenfield and R. Coching, Lawrence Erlbaum Associates, Inc., Publishers.

Seeley, David S. 1989. "A New Paradigm for Parent Involvement." *Educational Leadership* 47 (2): 46-48.

Shinn, Marybeth. 1978. "Father Absence and Children's Cognitive Development." *Psychological Bulletin* 85: 295-324.

Sizemore, B. A. 1987. "The Effective African American Elementary School." In *Schooling in Social Context: Qualitative Studies*, ed. G. Noblit and W. T. Pink. Norwood, N. J.: Ablex.

Spencer, B., M. Frankel, S. Ingels, K. Rasinski, and R. Tourangeau. 1990. *Base Year Sample Design Report*. Report prepared for the U.S. Department of Education. Washington, D.C.

Stevenson, David L., and David P. Baker. 1987. "The Family-School Relation and the Child's School Performance." *Child Development* 58:1348-1357.

Sweet, James A., and Larry Bumpass. 1987. *American Families and Households*. New York: Russell Sage Foundation.

Teachman, J. 1987. "Family Background, Educational Resources, and Educational Attainment." *American Sociological Review* 52:548-57.

Tuzlak, Aysan, and David W. Hillock. 1991. "Single Mothers and Their Children After Divorce: A Study of Those 'Who Make It'," In *Continuity and Change in Marriage and Family*, ed. Jean E. Veevers. Toronto, Canada: Holt, Rinehart and Winston of Canada, Ltd.

U.S. Department of Commerce. Bureau of the Census. 1991. *Statistical Abstract of the United States: 1991* (111th Edition). Washington, D.C.

U.S. Department of Commerce. 1990. *Current Population Reports*. Series P-20, No. 450. Washington, D.C.

U.S. Department of Education, Office of Educational Research and Improvement. 1989. *National Education Longitudinal Study of 1988: User's Manual, Base Year: Parent Component*.

U.S. Department of Education, Office of Educational Research and Improvement. 1989. *National Education Longitudinal Study of 1988: User's Manual, Base Year: Student Component*. NCES 90-464.

U.S. Department of Labor, Bureau of Labor Statistics. 1989. *Handbook of Labor Statistics, Bulletin 2340*. Washington, D.C.: Government Printing Office.

Van Galen, J. 1987. "Maintaining Control: The Structuring of Parental Involvement." In *Schooling in Social Context: Qualitative Studies*, ed. G. Noblit and W. T. Pink. Norwood, N. J.: Ablex.

About the Book and Editors

Parental involvement with children at home, in school, and in the community is one of the most important factors in educational success. Yet we know very little about the most effective approaches to parental intervention. Moreover, not all parents have the same resources or opportunities to act on the educational expectations they have for their children.

This book examines the resources available to parents and the actions parents can take to further their children's education. It is the first study of the subject based on major survey data, drawing from the National Education Longitudinal Study of 1988—a national survey of 26,000 eighth graders, their parents, teachers, and school administrators. The authors explore several important debates, including the extent to which parental involvement can mitigate the constraints of poverty for minorities and disadvantaged students, school choice and equality of educational opportunity, and the effects that school-sponsored activities involving parents have on educational performance.

Certain to change the thinking of educators and policymakers, this book is essential reading for scholars and parents as well.

Barbara Schneider is senior social scientist at the National Opinion Research Center and The University of Chicago. **James S. Coleman,** University Professor at The University of Chicago, is the author of many books on education and social theory.

Index